The Pre-Wrath Rapture of The Church: Is It Biblical?

The Pre-Wrath Rapture of The Church: Is It Biblical?

Paul S. Karleen

BF Press
P.O. Box L-601
Langhorne, PA 19047

THE PRE-WRATH RAPTURE OF THE CHURCH: IS IT BIBLICAL?

Copyright © 1991 by
Paul S. Karleen

Published by
BF Press
P.O. Box L-601
Langhorne, Pennsylvania 19047

Library of Congress Catalog Card Number: 90-92290

ISBN 0-9628612-0-0

All Scripture quotations, unless otherwise noted, are taken from *The New Scofield Reference Bible*, copyright © 1967 by Oxford University Press, Inc. Reprinted by permission.

Quotations from *The Pre-Wrath Rapture of the Church*, copyright © 1990 by Thomas Nelson Publishers, are used by permission.

Printed in the United States of America

Contents

Introduction

It's easy to play with words—our own or those of others. Sometimes we utter them for our own purposes, and sometimes we interpret words from others unfairly. When it comes to the Bible, we must be especially careful to determine what the authors, and the divine Author, intended it to mean. This book examines some words written about the Bible and some ways of interpreting biblical words.

I have written this book as an evaluation of a theological position that has recently been articulated in book form. I will take that book as representative of the view. It is not my intention to damage the author or other advocates of the position. However, I do firmly believe that it is essential to test, by the Bible itself, every statement that claims to be based on that Book. So, too, must others evaluate my work.

Unless otherwise indicated, all Scripture quotations are from the King James text as found in *The New Scofield Reference Bible*. References in parentheses are to pages in *The Pre-Wrath Rapture of the Church*. In order to avoid extensive footnoting, these are used in running text or at the point where a footnote number would ordinarily be found at the end of quoted material. For the sake of simplicity, the phrase "the author" is used of the writer of *The Pre-Wrath Rapture of the Church*.

My thanks go to the many friends who critiqued this book in manuscript form. I am indebted to them for their many valuable suggestions. I must record my special appreciation for the insight and unceasing support of Joy, my partner in ministry, and for the patience, encouragement, and help of my children, Daniel, Jessica, and Benjamin.

1

Will the Real
Rapture Please Stand Up?

I N THE EARLIER DAYS of American television, there was a popular program called "To Tell the Truth" on which four panelists were faced by three guests claiming to have an unusual profession. Two of the guests were impostors and could fool the panel, but the "real" one had to tell the truth. Panelists asked questions to determine which contestant was genuine, probing for weaknesses, inconsistencies, contradictions, gaps, and fibs. Viewers or panelists who knew the facts about the profession could often spot the fakers. When the questioning was over, the host, using the true guest's name would say, "Will the real . . . please stand up." After a little more faking by the guests, the true visitor rose to his feet. The audience loved it when the panelists were fooled.

The realm of biblical studies is very much like that quiz show. There are many people laying claim to being genuine, making statements that they say are true to the Bible. Often such statements are at odds with those of other people. Sometimes we wish there were an easy way to get the right view to stand up!

Unfortunately, not everything that people write or say about the Bible is true. There are many reasons for this. To begin with, interpreting the Bible can be very difficult. All of us run the risk of misunderstanding some parts. At times we impose our own preconceptions on it or skip important information. Some writers have good intentions, but are careless. Some are intentionally deceptive, some are naive, and some are inexperienced. Some present a lot of truth with a little error mixed in. Some, on the other hand, present a lot of error with just a little truth mixed in.

You have a responsibility before God to read and listen carefully and critically, checking the truth of everything you read about the Bible, everything a preacher or Bible teacher says, and even the contents of this book. You must ask, Which view is genuine? Which one matches what the Bible says? You have to be like the panelists on that show, probing for weaknesses and inconsistencies. In fact, the Bible tells us to do this in 2 Timothy 3:15 ("rightly dividing the word of truth") and in 1 Corinthians 14:29, where the Apostle Paul says that those in local church meetings were to check out the validity of what others said.

A New Book to Evaluate

In 1990 a book entitled *The Pre-Wrath Rapture of the Church*[1] appeared on the market. Its thesis is this: The Rapture of the Church of Jesus Christ will occur, not at the beginning of the seventieth week of Daniel, but sometime after its midpoint, just prior to the Day of the Lord. The Day of the Lord will be a time of wrath from God upon the inhabitants of the earth. Church-age believers will go through the first half of the seventieth week—three and one-half years—and more but will be spared the time of wrath.

People have wondered if the author is right. Can what he says be true? Does the Bible really say what he says it does? Perhaps some people, noting the author's sincerity and enthusiasm, have concluded that there must be at least some truth in his position.

On the other hand, some may wonder what all the fuss is about. Does it matter what we believe about the Rapture of the Church? After all, there are fine evangelicals such as those who do not believe that there will be a physical Millennium on the earth—these people are said to be "amillennial"—who make very little of the Rapture. And some people, pointing to the disagreements among believers, especially during this century, about the timing of the rapture, might throw up their hands in despair. "If theologians can't figure it out and can't agree, why should I bother with the matter?" they might say.

But the Rapture and its timing are very important, because they are a key part of God's plan of the ages. And while the Rapture, the Millennium, the seventieth week of Daniel, the second advent, and many other prophetic topics, are sometimes difficult to understand, every person who claims to walk with the God of Scripture should be a student of this topic and of biblical prophecy as a whole.

Perhaps you have already seen *The Pre-Wrath Rapture* and thought, Is there really something to this? Here is what everyone who reads *The Pre-Wrath Rapture of the Church* should ask: Is this book biblical? Does it really reflect what the Bible says? No matter how sincere and enthusiastic the author is, do his words really capture the facts of Scripture? You must be like one of those panelists, digging for the truth. Since you won't get the right view of the Rapture to stand up and announce its genuineness while the others remain seated, you will have to get at the truth yourself.

Some Important Components of Interpretation

I am convinced that the thesis of *The Pre-Wrath Rapture of the Church* is unbiblical because it involves many errors of interpretation. To gain our trust, a book that claims to set forth a unified description of such an important area of theology has to demonstrate the elements of sound interpretation. This book does not.

Are there any guidelines we can employ to help us get at the accuracy of this or any other theological position? Yes, there are. Here are four important components of biblical interpretation:

1. Correspondence to the facts
2. Accuracy concerning language
3. Attention to context
4. Logical consistency

In the following chapters I will examine many of the topics found in the book. While I cannot discuss every point the author makes, I will show that the major ones are seriously flawed, and I will do this in many cases by showing how he has erred in regard to facts, language, context, and logic. This is an entirely fair approach, because these are essential components of interpretation of the Bible, and the author of *The Pre-Wrath Rapture* claims to be doing biblical interpretation.

The words *fact, linguistic* or *language, context,* and *logic* occur many times in the author's argumentation. (See pp. 35, 313, etc. Please note that we are using the words *argument* and *argumentation* here to refer

11

to the way someone presents his case, not to angry exchange.) We have every right to see if he has the facts, has his linguistic data straight, looks at contexts, and uses sound logic. Over and over he says he is doing literal, straightforward interpretation of the Bible. Does he actually do that? He says he is a biblicist, but are his conclusions based on sound biblical interpretation?

There is no question that the author has wrestled with significant issues in biblical interpretation. He is convinced that the Rapture of the Church will not occur where the pretribulationist says it will. But while pretribulationism may have work to do on its position, should it be abandoned? More importantly, is the pre-wrath Rapture justified in its claim to be the true explanation of the unfolding of the seventieth week of Daniel and associated events? I believe the answer to both questions is a firm no.

The Basic Argumentation of *The Pre-Wrath Rapture*

No chain is any stronger than its weakest link, so even a chain with many links isn't necessarily strong. But often we are fooled by the bad logic of the fallacy of aggregation. We are impressed by numbers. Yet it is never true that putting together many bad arguments makes a good argument.

The author of *The Pre-Wrath Rapture* presents his position by adding one conclusion to another, in a chain-like effect. It is easy for the reader to think that the chain is sound and the conclusion is well supported, when actually they are not. Many of the links have serious flaws. But the book is written in such a way that, if the reader accepts each part (for example, as they are represented in the time and event charts), he is likely to conclude that the pre-wrath position is valid.

We can diagram the author's argumentation using letters to stand for conclusions. The reasoning proceeds this way:

> I assert that a is true.
> Partially on the basis of a, I assert that b is true.
> Partially on the basis of a and b, I assert that c is true.
> On the basis of a, b, and c, I assert that the conclusion is true.

In this kind of argumentation, the truth of the conclusion depends on all that precedes. But remember that many partial truths never make a whole truth. The total of anything can be no better than the quality of each of its components. If parts of the chain are wrong, the conclusion is false, since the argumentation toward the main conclusion proceeds by adding up subconclusions.

There are many complex arguments in *The Pre-Wrath Rapture*. It would take a very long book to analyze each one in detail. I have decided to analyze several key issues in the following chapters. Many of these issues or points bear on different parts of the author's argumentation. I will treat them approximately in the order in which they appear in the book.

The Purpose of This Book

I am not writing to defend a particular theological position or to compare the pre-wrath view with any other view. Instead, I will evaluate *The Pre-Wrath Rapture* on its own merits, especially with regard to its attention to facts, accuracy of linguistic detail, attention to context, and logic. I will make reference to particular theological positions only as necessary to clarify points.

The Object of Pre-Wrath Criticism

It may be helpful to some readers to have a quick summary of the main position that *The Pre-Wrath Rapture of the Church* is criticizing—the pretribulation Rapture of the Church. Most pretribulationists hold that the next event on the prophetic calendar is the Rapture of the Church of Christ before the beginning of the seven-year seventieth week described in Daniel 9:24-27. At the middle of that seventieth week, a thoroughly sinful world ruler, who has already come on the scene by that time, breaks a covenant he has made with Israel and begins a terrible persecution of that people. The Lord Jesus Christ returns bodily in glory at the end of the seventieth week to destroy nations gathered against Jerusalem and subsequently establishes His Millennial Kingdom on earth. That Kingdom is followed by the creation of the new heavens and new earth. The Day of the Lord commences at the beginning of the seventieth week and extends through the end of that Kingdom. Not all pretribulationists would hold to all of these details, and many would acknowledge that there are areas where work is necessary.

NOTES

1. Marvin Rosenthal, *The Pre-Wrath Rapture of the Church* (Nashville: Thomas Nelson Publishers, 1990).

2

When Does the Wrath of God Begin?

E VERY DAY we wrestle with determining the validity of information we receive. For example, we constantly wonder if TV and other media people really present us with the facts. Have they told us everything, or have they left something out? Has that salesman really represented his product fairly and accurately? Parents expect their children to tell the truth, and every Christian must tell the truth and encourage others to do the same. Of course, this is especially important when we study the Bible and when we read what others say about the Bible. Is the writer leaving anything out? Is he or she giving it to us straight?

This isn't very difficult to determine. If we take the time, we can usually learn what the facts are by looking carefully at the Bible. Sometimes the facts are hard to get at, as when biblical languages are involved, since most people don't know how to work with them. Nevertheless, objective information is available. For example, if someone says that a particular Greek word occurs 29 times in the New Testament, that can be easily verified—at least by someone. Or if you read, "The Bible never says 'do not lie,'" you might have to look a while, but you could eventually determine if that is true. Verifying the facts is the first place to start in understanding the Scriptures.

According to the pre-wrath view, God's wrath on the earth doesn't start until the Day of the Lord, after the six seals of Revelation 6, and after cosmic disturbances. The Church is raptured just before the beginning of wrath, since, according to 1 Thessalonians 5:9, believers of this age are not appointed to wrath. However, according to the author, the Church will go through the events of the first six seals. While the first six seals involve great difficulties for people on the earth, they do not involve God's wrath (pp. 140, 171, etc.). In addition, the Tribulation is only the first part of the second half of the seventieth week and contains no wrath (pp. 104, 105). It is very important to the pre-wrath position that wrath not begin until after the middle of the seventieth week of Daniel, after the Tribulation, after the first six seals, after the cosmic disturbances, and after the Rapture. Please note that the time of the beginning of wrath, the meaning and timing of the seals, the start of the Day of the Lord, the time of the Rapture, and cosmic disturbances are all connected. Those who hold to a pretribulation Rapture associate all these events, too, but place them at different times. A simple chart of the pre-wrath view will help at this point.

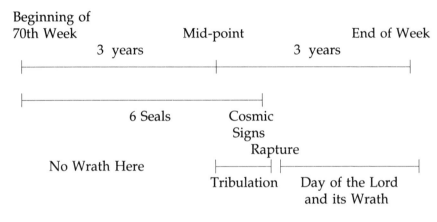

Does the Bible really teach that there is no wrath during the Tribulation or before the Day of the Lord? If it does, then perhaps the pre-wrath Rapture is right. But if it doesn't, then one of the main points of the position is invalid. Let's see what the biblical facts are.

Luke's Evidence

The author correctly looks to the Olivet Discourse and Matthew 24 for events of the seventieth week of Daniel. We know that he views Matthew 24 and Luke 21 as parallel in their description of these events (p. 152). A glance at any harmony of the Gospels will show the great similarity in language between Matthew and Luke in their recording of the Olivet Discourse.[1] They *are* parallel. But has the author read the evidence accurately? He states many times that the

16

Tribulation is not a time of God's wrath. In addition, he stresses that the period of the seals does not contain wrath (pp. 171-172).

> Wrath is restricted to the latter part of the seventieth week, specifically the Day of the Lord period. (p. 172)

> God's wrath does not start until the opening of the seventh seal. (p. 172)

But what does Luke say? In 21:23 he records Jesus' words as follows:

> But woe unto them that are with child, and to them that nurse children, in those days! For there shall be great distress in the land, and wrath upon this people.

We observe the following:

1. In looking at a harmony of the Gospels we see that Luke 21:23 is parallel to Matthew 24:19-22. They describe the same time period. Matthew refers to this time as one that has "great tribulation" (v. 21). While there are some who interpret Luke 21:20-24 as referring to the destruction of Jerusalem in 70 A.D., there are many reasons for interpreting the passage as referring to (1) the end times only or (2) the end times and 70 A.D.

   a. Luke 21:22 indicates that the events of verses 20-24 (and perhaps more) are the "fulfillment of all that has been written." This is undoubtedly a reference to the Old Testament predictions of the end times and would include such passages as Hosea 9:7-9. It is unlikely that verse 22 would be connecting the wide scope of Old Testament prophecies ("all things") with only the destruction of Jerusalem in 70 A.D.

   b. There are several striking correspondences between Luke 21:10-14, Matthew 24:15-19, and Mark 13:14-17. These involve the ordering of ideas and exact word correspondences, such as *desolation* in Luke 21:20, Matthew 24:15, and Mark. 13:14. It is very likely that Luke preserves Jesus' words concerning (1) Jerusalem (v. 20), (2) punishment, distress, and wrath (v. 22), and (3) the times of the Gentiles (v. 24) as they appeared at this point in the actual Olivet Discourse. These are words that Matthew and Luke omit. The alternative is that Jesus spoke about Jerusalem's destruction at another point in the discourse, and Luke moved it here. This would not be an unusual feature, as disclosed by comparison of the synoptic Gospels. But it would mean that Jesus would have used, at another point, the words and phrases contained in Matthew and Luke. If these words were spoken in the Olivet Discourse where Luke has them, they must fit with Matthew and Mark's setting. Matthew and Mark are clearly speaking of the end times and not of 70 A.D., as indicated particularly by Matthew 24:15/Mark 13:14 and Matthew 24:23-31/Mark. 13:21-27. It is highly likely, then, that Luke 21:20-24 has an end-time reference. There is nothing in the passage that does not fit with that time. For example, we know that during the end times Jerusalem will be a focal point of attack by the enemies of Israel.

c. In addition, Jesus may be speaking of 70 A.D. at the same time. The description in verse 20 of the surrounding of Jerusalem certainly fits with that time, but it is not likely that verse 22 ("fulfillment of all that has been written") was totally fulfilled at that time.

Thus, the wrath of Luke 21:23, while perhaps applying also to 70 A.D., at least has reference to the end times. And, as indicated by the sequence of Luke in comparison with Matthew and Mark, the wrath comes during the time of tribulation (Mt. 24:21/Mark 13:19). In addition to all of this, we should note that the author places Luke 21:23-25 in the seventieth week (p. 152).

2. It is significant that Luke 21:23*a* and *b* are connected by the word "for" (the Greek word *gar*), which provides an explanation. Verse 23*b* gives an explanation of the events of 23*a* and must take place at the same time, not sometime later. The woe exists because of the wrath. Thus, Luke teaches that there will be wrath during the time that Matthew describes as having "great tribulation."

3. The author says that the Day of the Lord, in his view the only time of wrath, will be a period of chastening and purifying for Israel (p. 175). But Luke 21:23 has "wrath upon this people"—wrath coming on Jews. He uses *orgē*, the same word used in Revelation and normally translated "wrath" and the word that the author interprets as describing the wrath of God. The author insists that *wrath* is never used in Revelation of the period of the first six seals. But Luke places

it (using the same word) before the cosmic events of the sixth seal, thus teaching that "in those days" (which the author takes to be the tribulation of Matthew 24:19 [p. 205]) there will be wrath on Israel.

4. The author says that the Olivet Discourse is sequential in progression (p. 60). He also asserts by his chart (p. 152) that Luke 21:25 is parallel to the sixth seal, and is, therefore, before any wrath. But Luke 21 has wrath before this.

5. To put it in terms of the cosmic events, Luke 21:25 records the cosmic disturbances, so wrath comes on Israel before the disturbances.

Lest someone think that Luke is not parallel to Matthew here, please note the language of the following pairs:

Luke 21	Matthew 24
v. 21 Then let them who are in Judaea flee to the mountains	v. 16 Then let them who are in Judaea flee into the mountains
v. 23 But woe unto them that are with child....For there shall be great distress in the land, and wrath upon this people	v. 19 And woe unto those that are with child
v. 25 And there shall be signs in the sun, and in the moon, and in the stars	v. 29 Immediately after the tribulation of those days shall the sun be darkened, and the moon shall not give its light, and the stars shall fall from heaven.

Luke's sequence is the same as Matthew's.

Let's summarize at this point. Luke says there will be wrath during the period when the author says there will not be wrath. Who is right? I'll go along with Luke. It might be helpful to lay out the main elements sequentially, comparing Luke and the author's view of Matthew 24.

Luke 21	_Pre-Wrath_ view of Matthew 24
Luke 21 is tribulation	Matthew 24 is tribulation (assumes the Olivet Discourse is chronological)
v. 23a woe on mothers	v. 19 woe on mothers
v. 23b wrath on Israel	v. 21 tribulation
v. 25 cosmic disturbances	v. 29 cosmic disturbances, opening of the sixth seal as prelude to the Day of the Lord, then the Rapture and the beginning of wrath on Israel
	Wrath does not begin until here

Conclusion

On page 176 the author quotes David Cooper:

> When the plain sense of Scripture makes common sense, seek no other sense; therefore, take every word at its primary, ordinary, usual, literal meaning unless the facts of the immediate context, studied in the light of related passages and axiomatic and fundamental truths, indicate clearly otherwise.[2]

Indeed, we should opt for "the plain sense of Scripture." The text of Luke is clear. There is wrath during the period where the author of _Pre-Wrath_ places the Tribulation, during the period where he places the six seals, before the seventh seal, before his cosmic disturbances, before where he places the Rapture, and before his Day of the Lord starts—all times when he says there cannot be wrath. We are observing a serious error of fact. For whatever reason, the author did not take Luke 21:23 into account.

Make no mistake about it, the timing of wrath is the cornerstone of the pre-wrath position. In fact, the author tells us his most important purpose for writing.

> The objective of this volume is to demonstrate that the
> Day of the Lord is the time of divine wrath. (p. 35)

Luke's Olivet account thus destroys the crucial element in the author's argument. He cannot restrict wrath to the Day of the Lord and be true to the Bible.

NOTES

1. For example, A. T. Robertson, *A Harmony of the Gospels for Students of the Life of Christ* (New York: Harper and Row, 1950) and Robert L. Thomas and Stanley N. Gundry, eds., *The NIV Harmony of the Gospels* (San Francisco: Harper and Row, 1987).

2. David L. Cooper, *An Exposition of the Book of Revelation* (Los Angeles: Biblical Research Society, 1972), p. 9.

3

Are There Blessings
During the Day of the Lord?

T HE WORD *context* means surroundings and is very significant to biblical understanding. The Bible contains many pieces of information, all of which come in contexts. If we don't pay attention to contexts, we can easily get the information wrong.

This is true in all human communication. For example, if I said to my wife, "I'm going to the bank," and I have just said, "Do you have any checks you'd like to deposit?" she would conclude that I am going to our local financial institution. But if I have just said, "I'm looking for my pole," she would conclude I was going to the river bank to do some fishing. Context is of great importance in interpreting anything we say or write.

We must be sure that people pay attention to the context of portions of the text of the Bible. If they let the texts fit with their surroundings, then it is more likely that their conclusion about meaning is valid. But if they look at words and verses in isolation, ignoring the surroundings (intentionally or unintentionally), what they say has a high likelihood of being wrong. We will see that this is exactly what the author of *The Pre-Wrath Rapture* does.

Inconsistencies

The pre-wrath position asserts that the Day of the Lord is exclusively a time of the outpouring of God's wrath, not of God's favor.

> There is no blessing associated with the Day of the Lord in the texts that describe it. (p. 128)

The description of the Day of the Lord in the Old Testament is exclusively a time of devastating judgment. No blessing is associated with it. When blessing is mentioned, it is only incidental and given as a chronological marker (for example, after the Day of the Lord there will be blessing, Isa. 11; 35; 60). (p. 127)

The author indicates that some Bible teachers say that the Day of the Lord will include "darkness and light, judgment and blessing, night and day" and that the Day continues through the Millennium (p. 126). In response to this, he says that the ending point of the Day is not crucial to his argument. But then he goes on to attempt to show that the Day contains no blessing and does not include the Millennium. He quotes with approval Richard Mayhue:

The prominent theme of the Day of the Lord prophecies is God's judgment for sin. It is present in every Day of the Lord passage. The blessings of Christ's Millennial reign are subsequent to and as a result of the Day of the Lord, but they are not part of it.[1] (p. 128)

In addition he says concerning the Millennium,

The supposed exegetical basis for extending the Day of the Lord through the Millennium rests solely on one verse of Scripture. (p. 128)

There simply is no biblical basis for making millennial texts that speak of "in that day" part of an extended Day of the Lord. (p. 129)

It is not difficult to demonstrate that the author is inconsistent with himself. Remember that he says concerning the Day of the Lord,

No blessing is associated with it. (p. 127)

There is no blessing associated with the Day of the Lord in the texts that describe it. (p. 128)

However, he admits that there is some kind of favor from God associated with the Day of the Lord. After quoting Joel 1:15; 2:1-2, 10-11, and 30-31 as passages that refer to the Day as a time of judgment, he allows for blessing "at the end," as indicated by 3:14-16. In regard to this passage he says,

> At the end of the Day of the Lord, a surviving remnant
> will be gloriously saved . . . . (p. 119)

Yet he says that we should not interpret this to mean that there is
blessing during the Day of the Lord. This is not simply a matter of
terminology. He contradicts his own statements to the effect that no
blessing is "associated with" the Day of the Lord. There *is* blessing
"associated with" the Day of the Lord.

Errors of Fact and Context

Let's assume that the author's main interest is in showing that
there is no blessing during the Day of the Lord. This would mean, for
him, that the Day of the Lord stops before the Kingdom. Is this true?
Does the Bible really teach this? It is not difficult to show that it does
not. The author quotes several Old Testament passages that refer to
the Day of the Lord. In many instances he italicizes the word *day* and
associated words (pp. 119-123). Here are some of the phrases that he
interprets as referring to the same time period:

> a day
> the day
> the day of the Lord
> day of the Lord
> in that day

There can be no question that he views these phrases as clues to
identify which passages speak of the Day of the Lord. He cautions the
reader not to assume that all uses of *day* can be taken to refer to the
Day of the Lord. That is reasonable. But let's look at several texts that
speak of the Day of the Lord or describe the same events.

1. Joel 2-3

a. The sequence of events

Here is the text of Joel 2:30-3:2:

> (2:30) And I will show wonders in the heavens and in the
> earth: blood, and fire, and pillars of smoke.

> (2:31) The sun shall be turned into darkness, and the moon into blood, before the great and the terrible day of the LORD come.
>
> (2:32) And it shall come to pass that whosoever shall call on the name of the LORD shall be delivered; for in Mount Zion and in Jerusalem shall be deliverance, as the LORD hath said, and in the remnant whom the LORD shall call.
>
> (3:1) For, behold, in those days, and in that time, when I shall bring again the captivity of Judah and Jerusalem,
>
> (3:2) I will also gather all nations, and will bring them down into the Valley of Jehoshaphat, and will judge them there for my people and for my heritage, Israel, whom they have scattered among the nations, and parted my land.

We should note first that Joel 2:32 and 3:1 are right in the middle of a passage that the author has cited as describing the Day of the Lord. He indicates that 1:15; 2:1-2, 10-11, and 30-31, as well as 3:14-16, describe the Day of the Lord (p. 119). Please remember that in the pre-wrath position the cosmic signs come just before the Day of the Lord. Joel describes that in 2:30-31. The next thing he describes is blessing! In addition, 3:1 is explicit that blessing comes at the same time. There is no justification for relegating this to another time. The blessing may come after judgment, but it is still within the Day of the Lord.

Let's lay out the sequence of this passage.

2:30 and 31	cosmic signs
2:32	salvation
3:1	restoration of Judah and Jerusalem's fortunes "in that time"
3:2	judgment on the nations

There is no escaping the meaning of Joel in this passage. Blessing comes during the same time period as the cosmic signs and judgment on the nations—an impossible combination for the pre-wrath position!

b. New Testament evidence

The New Testament provides an interesting confirmation of what we have just seen. It is significant that in Acts 2 Peter quotes extensively from Joel 2. Such quotations from the Old Testament in the New Testament are always significant. In Acts 2:20-21 Peter quotes Joel 2:28-32*a* as pertaining to the same period of time. Joel 2:30 clearly contains cosmic changes, which the author of *The Pre-Wrath Rapture* repeatedly connects with the Day of the Lord. Peter, however, tells us that verse 32 is part of the same time period. Coming, as it does, as part of Scripture inspired by the Holy Spirit, this New Testament passage provides God's interpretation of Joel 2. Once again, we see that there is blessing during the time period of the Day of the Lord. The author has made errors of fact and has not taken into account the surroundings of verses.

2. Zephaniah 3

Let's examine a second significant Old Testament passage, Zephaniah 3:8-13*a*.

> (8) Therefore, wait upon me, saith the LORD, until the day that I rise up to the prey; for my determination is to gather the nations, that I may assemble the kingdoms, to pour upon them mine indignation, even all my fierce anger; for all the earth shall be devoured with the fire of my jealousy.
>
> (9) For then will I turn to the peoples a pure language, that they may all call upon the name of the LORD, to serve him with one consent.
>
> (10) From beyond the rivers of Ethiopia my suppliants, even the daughter of my dispersed, shall bring mine offering.
>
> (11) In that day shalt thou not be ashamed for all thy doings, in which thou hast transgressed against me; for then I will take away out of the midst of thee those who rejoice in thy pride, and thou shalt no more be haughty in my holy mountain.
>
> (12) I will also leave in the midst of thee an afflicted and poor people, and they shall trust in the name of the LORD.
>
> (13) The remnant of Israel shall not do iniquity, nor speak lies, neither shall a deceitful tongue be found in their mouth; for they shall feed and lie down, and none shall make them afraid.

To be sure, this portion of Zephaniah does not contain the phrase "Day of the Lord." But the author cites 3:8 as describing events during the Day of the Lord (pp. 13, 124). Therefore, by his own assertion, this is a Day of the Lord passage. Yet, contrary to his basic thesis, verses 12-13 describe a period of spiritual and physical blessing for a remnant of Israel. Again, the author demonstrates errors of fact and context. Interestingly, he is inconsistent, because he says elsewhere (p. 146) that Zephaniah 3:8 applies to the time after the Day of the Lord, his extended 30-day period.

3. Isaiah 34 and 35

Following is a third Old Testament passage, Isaiah 34:2ff., partially abbreviated and with observations interspersed:

> (34:2) For the indignation of the LORD is upon all nations, and his fury upon all their armies; he hath utterly destroyed them, he hath delivered them to the slaughter.

The author cites verse 2 as describing God's divine wrath during the Day of the Lord (p. 124).

> (34:4) And all the host of heaven shall be dissolved, and the heavens shall be rolled together like a scroll; and all their host shall fall down, as the leaf falleth off from the vine, and like a falling fig from the fig tree.

This describes cosmic disturbances. The author cites verse 4 as referring to the Day of the Lord (p. 124).

> (34:8) For it is the day of the LORD's vengeance, and the year of recompenses for the controversy of Zion.

The author cites verse 8 as describing the Day of the Lord (p. 124).

> (35:1) The wilderness and the solitary place shall be glad for them; and the desert shall rejoice, and blossom like the rose.
> (35:2) It shall blossom abundantly, and rejoice even with joy and singing; the glory of Lebanon shall be given unto it, the excellency of Carmel and Sharon; they shall see the glory of the LORD and the excellency of our God.

27

(35:3) Strengthen the weak hands, and confirm the feeble knees.
(35:4) Say to those who are of a fearful heart, Be strong, fear not; behold, your God will come with vengeance, even God, with a recompense; he will come and save you.
(35:5) Then the eyes of the blind shall be opened, and the ears of the deaf shall be unstopped.
(35:6) Then shall the lame man leap as an hart, and the tongue of the dumb sing; for in the wilderness shall waters break out, and streams in the desert.

This passage moves from judgment to blessing to judgment to blessing. The time of the divine healing in 35:5 and 6 is indicated by the use, at the beginning of 35:5, of the Hebrew word 'az, which could also be translated "at that time."[2] Verses 1, 5, and 6 are not introduced with any words indicating that the blessing comes at a different time. Therefore, in a passage that the author says describes the Day of the Lord, we find interwoven descriptions of blessing and judgment.

4. Haggai 2

Let's look at portions of Haggai 2:6ff.

(2:6) For thus saith the LORD of hosts: Yet once, it is a little while, and I will shake the heavens, and the earth, and the sea, and the dry land;

This must be a description of what the author interprets elsewhere as events at the beginning of the Day of the Lord.

(2:7) And I will shake all nations, and the desire of all nations shall come; and I will fill this house with glory, saith the LORD of hosts.
(2:21) Speak to Zerubbabel, governor of Judah, saying, I will shake the heavens and the earth;
(2:23) In that day, saith the LORD of hosts, will I take thee, O Zerubbabel, my servant, the son of Shealtiel, saith the LORD, and will make thee as a signet; for I have chosen thee, saith the LORD of hosts.

In 2:7a we have God's anger against the nations. Again, for the author this is part of the Day of the Lord. But 7b describes the glorious transformation of the Temple. Note that this is effected through the coming of the "desire of all nations," the Lord Jesus Christ. In 2:21 we see the same description of the shaking of the nations as in verses 6 and 7. Then verse 23 tells us that Zerubbabel, apparently resurrected, will be blessed by God. This occurs "in that day" or "on that day." This phrase is used often in Hebrew to describe a particular day or definite time (Gen. 15:18 and 33:16). It is used very often in prophecy as a formula in describing what is to come at a time of future blessing and retribution, as in Amos 8:3, 9; Hosea 2:18, 20, 23; and Isaiah 2:11, 17, and 20.[3]

Please note that in this passage in Haggai we see blessings on Israel coming during the time period that the author views as belonging to the Day of the Lord. In addition, the phrase "in that day" is the same one used in Isaiah 2. The author assigns Isaiah 2:12-21 to the Day of the Lord.

It is significant that the author says that Charles Ryrie is too loose with his use of *day* to identify actual Day of the Lord passages (pp. 128, 129). Yet he himself repeatedly italicizes *that day* and applies it to the Day of the Lord. While Haggai does not use the phrase "Day of the Lord," he describes events that the author interprets as part of the Day and uses the same phrase as Isaiah 2. Thus we are justified, on the author's own grounds, in seeing Haggai as describing not only (1) the Day of the Lord itself, but also (2) a time of blessing that occurs during the same time period as the judgments. It is interesting that while the author criticizes others for using *in that day* as an automatic clue for identifying the Day of the Lord, he includes in his description of the events of the Day some passages that do not at all contain the word *day* in any of its combinations with other words, e.g., Isaiah 34:1-2 (p. 124). He does not indicate how he decided which verses refer to the Day of the Lord.

5. Zechariah 12-14

Let's look at a fifth Old Testament passage, portions of Zechariah 12:2-14:20. This may be the most telling in relation to the author's position.

> (12:2) Behold, I will make Jerusalem a cup of trembling unto all the peoples round about, when they shall be in the siege both against Judah and against Jerusalem.

(12:3) And in that day will I make Jerusalem a burdensome stone for all peoples; all that burden themselves with it shall be cut in pieces, though all the nations of the earth be gathered together against it.

(12:4) In that day, saith the LORD, I will smite every horse with terror, and his rider with madness; and I will open mine eyes upon the house of Judah, and will smite every horse of the peoples with blindness.

(12:6) In that day will I make the governors of Judah like an hearth of fire among the wood, and like a torch of fire in a sheaf; and they shall devour all the peoples round about, on the right hand and on the left; and Jerusalem shall be inhabited again in her own place, even in Jerusalem.

(12:7) The LORD also shall save the tents of Judah first, that the glory of the house of David and the glory of the inhabitants of Jerusalem do not magnify themselves against Judah.

(12:8) In that day shall the LORD defend the inhabitants of Jerusalem; and he that is feeble among them at that day shall be like David; and the house of David shall be like God, like the angel of the LORD before them.

(12:9) And it shall come to pass, in that day, that I will seek to destroy all the nations that come against Jerusalem.

(12:10) And I will pour upon the house of David, and upon the inhabitants of Jerusalem, the Spirit of grace and of supplications; and they shall look upon me whom they have pierced, and they shall mourn for him, as one mourneth for his only son, and shall be in bitterness for him, as one that is in bitterness for his firstborn.

(12:11) In that day shall there be a great mourning in Jerusalem, as the mourning of Hadadrimmon, in the Valley of Megiddon.

(13:1) In that day there shall be a fountain opened to the house of David and to the inhabitants of Jerusalem for sin and for uncleanness.

(13:2) And it shall come to pass, in that day, saith the Lord of hosts, that I will cut off the names of the idols out of the land, and they shall no more be remembered; and also I will cause the prophets and the unclean spirit to pass out of the land.

(14:1) Behold, the day of the LORD cometh, and thy spoil shall be divided in the midst of thee.

(14:2) For I will gather all nations against Jerusalem to battle; and the city shall be taken, and the houses rifled, and the women ravished; and half of the city shall go forth into captivity, and the residue of the people shall not be cut off from the city.

(14:4) And his feet shall stand in that day upon the Mount of Olives, which is before Jerusalem on the east, and the Mount of Olives shall cleave in its midst toward the east and toward the west, and there shall be a very great valley; and half of the mountain shall remove toward the north, and half of it toward the south.

(14:6) And it shall come to pass, in that day, that the light shall not be clear, nor dark,

(14:8) And it shall be, in that day, that living waters shall go out from Jerusalem; half of them toward the former sea, and half of them toward the hinder sea; in summer and in winter shall it be.

(14:9) And the LORD shall be king over all the earth; in that day shall there be one LORD, and his name one.

(14:20) In that day shall there be upon the bells of the horses, HOLINESS UNTO THE LORD; and the pots in the LORD's house shall be like the bowls before the altar.

A face-value approach to this portion of Scripture reveals that it teaches judgment and blessing in the same "day." Yet the author says the following:

1. 12:8-9 refer to the Kingdom (after his "Day")
2. 12:9 refers to a 30-day period after the Day of the Lord
3. 14:1-4 refer to the Day of the Lord proper.

Concerning 14:1-4 he states,

The prophet Zechariah, who foretold the cataclysmic events that are to befall the city of Jerusalem, added this crucial testimony concerning the Day of the Lord. (p. 122)

31

Please observe (1) the number of times the phrase "in that day" occurs, and (2) that it occurs in reference to judgment and blessing. In fact, 14:1-4, which the author says describe the Day of the Lord, are intimately linked with subsequent verses that describe blessings that occur "in that day." There is no biblical justification whatsoever for separating judgment and blessing statements in this passage as belonging to different eras. They are all part of the Day of the Lord. I encourage the reader to examine all of the passages I have referred to in this section to determine personally whether or not blessings are interspersed with wrath and judgment. I believe that no other conclusion can be reached than that the Day of the Lord includes blessing.

The biblical picture of the Day of the Lord certainly stresses the judgment of God. The Old Testament in particular does this in order to emphasize for Israel that, at the great time of the manifestation of God's activity in relation to Israel, blessings will not come until the nation has been purified. Israel looked for the blessings without a reckoning with national and individual sin. However, the Day of the Lord passages do include blessings, particularly as part of the Kingdom to follow the time of judgment on the earth. But remember that the author stresses, "There are no blessings associated with the Day of the Lord," and "When blessing is mentioned, it is only incidental . . . ."

We will examine 2 Peter 3:10ff. at length in the next chapter. But we should note that in regard to the Day of the Lord and 2 Peter 3:10 the author states,

> *The supposed exegetical basis for extending the Day of the Lord through the Millennium rests solely on one verse of Scripture.* (p. 128)

We have seen several passages in the Old Testament that teach otherwise.

Conclusion

In regard to the duration of the Day of the Lord, the author has committed errors of fact and context. The Bible does teach that there is blessing during the Day of the Lord. The author's central contention that there is no blessing—only wrath—associated with the Day of the Lord is incorrect.

NOTES

1. Richard Mayhue, "The Prophet's Watchword: The Day of the Lord," unpublished doctoral diss. (Winona Lake, IN: Grace Theological Seminary, 1981), p. 93.

2. Francis Brown, S. R. Driver, and Charles A. Briggs, *A Hebrew and English Lexicon of the Old Testament* (Oxford: Oxford University Press, 1962), p. 23.

3. Brown, Driver, and Briggs, p. 400.

4

Second Peter 3 and the Day of the Lord

WE HAVE ALL HEARD or used the phrase, "That's not logical." When we say that, we are expressing our belief that the pieces aren't all present, or that someone isn't expressing himself clearly. We are not saying that a person is not mentally competent. For many centuries philosophers have wrestled with what it means to be logical. They've concluded that being logical is simply reasoning well. A person who reasons along commonly accepted lines is logical. Here is an example of good and bad logic:

Good: All men are males.
John is a man.
Therefore, John is a male.

Bad: All men are males.
My dog Fido is a male.
Therefore, Fido is a man.

I'm sure you were able to see through the second example.

When someone attacks his opponent's character, background, or appearance, and not his ideas or words, he is committing the logical fallacy of the attack against the person, also known as the *ad hominem* argument. He may win the day with his argumentation, but he is not using accepted logic.

Subtly or overtly threatening another person's welfare in order to prevail in a discussion involves the logical fallacy of the *appeal to force*. Again, the arguer may prevail, but he has not used good logic. If a father tells his daughter to clean her room because if she doesn't he will not allow her go to a crucial ball game, he has used the appeal to force. On the other hand, explaining why she should clean her room would involve sound logic. Of course, this may not get dad what he wants, but it's good logic!

Reasoning that does not use data to advance an argument is called *circular reasoning* or *begging the question*.[1] This can take several forms, some of which are (1) repeating a claim without bringing forth new data; (2) repeating a claim without allowing data to speak (that is, finding what one claims is true while suppressing evidence); (3) restating a claim in different words without new data.

For example, if someone tells me that it is raining, and I ask him how he knows, and he says, "Because it's raining," he is guilty of circular logic. Giving a claim a second time does not constitute proof or support for the first occurrence. In other words, I requested support for the claim, and all I got was a repetition of the same claim. If there is data, it should be allowed to speak.

Here's another way to look at it. If a friend tells me that all ducks are white, and then a black duck appears, and his response is that the animal cannot be a duck since all ducks are white, he has committed the logical fallacy of circular argumentation; he has ignored the evidence.

This is what we saw in the previous chapter in the arbitrary distinctions as to which passages speak of the Day of the Lord and which do not. We observed that in at least five major passages (which by the author's own admission refer to the Day of the Lord) there is blessing woven in with judgments. Since he believes that no Day of the Lord verses can have blessings, he assigns to another time period those that run counter to his assumption.

Many theologians and literary critics involved in the study of principles of interpretation have underscored the need for objectivity with regard to any text that is being examined. British biblical scholar Graham Stanton phrases it this way:

> The interpreter must allow his own presuppositions and his own pre-understanding to be modified or even completely reshaped by the text itself . . . . There must be constant dialogue between the interpreter and the text.[2]

The American literary critic E. D. Hirsch, Jr. says similarly,

> When an interpreter maintains his unruffled certainty in the face of contrary opinions, we may assume that he...has fallen victim to the self-confirmability of interpretations.[3]

The interpreter's determination to entertain alternative hypotheses about his text . . . is the necessary precondition for objective judgment.[4]

These quotes all say essentially the same thing: We must always pay attention to the evidence.

The Logical Errors

The text of 2 Peter 3:10 poses a serious problem for the pre-wrath position because it indicates that (1) the Day of the Lord extends through the destruction of the physical universe and the creation of the new heavens and new earth, and (2) righteousness will find a home during the Day of the Lord. Although early in the book the author asserts that he will not attempt to erect any straw men and then argue against them, he does just that in his discussion of 2 Peter 3, misstating the position of the pretribulationist.

Most premillennialists interpret 2 Peter 3:10-13 as describing events before the Millennium (the coming "as a thief") and after it (reshaping of the heavens and earth), with the Day of the Lord extending through the creation of the new heavens and new earth and including judgment as well as blessing. Recall that one of the main supports for the author's view that the Day of the Lord cannot cover the period of the Millennium is that it cannot contain blessing, which he acknowledges is part of the Millennium. But in the preceding chapter we showed that many times in the prophets the blessings of the Millennium are included in the Day of the Lord. After stating the pretribulational view, the author brings in his assumption that the Day cannot extend through the Millennium and says the pretribulationist must then be forced to espouse the view (which the author himself has created) that there are two Day eras. Then he proceeds to prove this view wrong.

He states that the phrase "Where is the promise of his coming?" (3:4) makes no sense if applied to a Day before the Millennium and a separate Day afterward. This two-Day view is not the position of the pretribulationist. The author has created it. The pretribulationist does not try to argue for two occurrences of the Day of the Lord. The author creates that position, and then argues against it. When he believes he has shown that it is false, he concludes that he has shown that his view is right—that 2 Peter 3 must refer to the one Day of the Lord that he thinks occurs during the seventieth week of Daniel. Thus the author creates a straw man, attempts to disprove it, and then asserts that his position is vindicated. This is an evident fallacy.

A second logical fallacy is also involved. In saying that if Peter is speaking of a Day at the end of the Kingdom, there must be two distinct Days (p. 129), the author commits the fallacy of the *false dilemma*, in which too few choices are offered. It is seen in the classical joke, "Have you stopped beating your wife?" Here the answerer has no way out. No matter whether he answers yes or no, he incriminates himself. A viable alternative in this case, of course, is that Peter describes a unitary period of time from the start of the Day at the beginning of the seventieth week to the creation of the new heavens and new earth.

The Linguistic Errors

The Bible's authors originally wrote in three languages: Hebrew, Aramaic, and Greek. Conservative biblical scholars are agreed that the most accurate interpretive work can only be done by working with the original languages. While there are many good translations available today, they do not have all the information we need when we are trying to determine and summarize what the Bible says.

All sound interpreters of the Bible must possess accurate understanding of the original languages. They may not be teachers of Hebrew, Aramaic, or Greek, but they must know some basic things about how biblical languages work and be able to use available reference material accurately. Commenting on the place of language in biblical interpretation, and using the word *exegesis* as essentially equivalent to *interpretation,* British scholar F. F. Bruce has said,

> There can be no true biblical theology unless it is based on sound biblical exegesis, and there can be no sound biblical exegesis unless a firm textual and grammatical foundation has been laid for it.[5]

The word *linguistic* is often used as an adjective to talk about things that have to do with language. It is also used in a narrower sense to refer to the scientific study of language. In this book we will be using *linguistic* only in the first sense.

The author states concerning his erected two-day view,

> The prophets knew nothing of that. They spoke of the Day of the Lord with the definite article—they knew of only one such event. (p. 129)

There are two linguistic errors here. First, Hebrew did not need a definite article with a noun in order to have that noun refer to one particular item. English is like Hebrew in this respect. For example, if I say, "I see a chair in the middle of the room," you understand immediately that I am referring to one particular chair. It is not necessary to have the word *the* present in English or in Hebrew to communicate singularity. His understanding of the use of the Hebrew article is incorrect.

But of even greater significance is his statement that the prophets spoke of the Day of the Lord using the definite article. The phrase "Day of the Lord" occurs in the Old Testament 18 times. Following are the occurrences:

Isaiah	2:12	Amos	5:18 (twice)
	13:6		5:20
	13:9	Obadiah	15
Ezekiel	13:5	Zephaniah	1:7
	30:3		1:14
Joel	1:15	Zechariah	14:1 (has *great*
	2:1		*day of the Lord*
	2:11		and *day of the*
	2:31		*Lord*)
	3:14	Malachi	4:5

The intention of the Old Testament writers can be identified in this case only by looking at the Hebrew text. The use of an article in a translation does not give us enough information. An examination of the Hebrew text for each of these verses reveals that the article never occurs with the Hebrew word translated "day." The reader who is acquainted with the Hebrew text can verify this directly. Other readers may have access to an interlinear text. I am not arguing that there are two periods known as the Day of the Lord. Rather, I am attempting to show that the author's refutation of that position (his straw man) on the basis of the Hebrew article has no legitimate basis. Thus the author has committed the logical fallacy of the straw man, as well as factual and linguistic errors.

The Nature of the Destruction in 2 Peter 3

In arguing against Peter's inclusion of events after the Millennium in the Day of the Lord, the author attempts to show that the events of 3:10-13 simply describe a reshaping of the earth prior to the Kingdom of Christ. An examination of the Greek text of this passage will show his error. Here is 2 Peter 3:10:

> But the day of the Lord will come as a thief in the night, in which the heavens shall pass away with a great noise, and the elements shall melt with fervent heat; the earth also, and the works that are in it, shall be burned up.

The author states that Peter's description of what happens to the earth is parallel to what happened during the flood.

> He is not talking of total annihilation of the earth any more than the earth perishing in the days of Noah was total annihilation. He is talking of nonannihilative judgment during the Day of the Lord as the prophets foretold, but in connection with Christ's return before the Millennium begins. (p. 130)

However, the text actually shows that Peter speaks of the two events quite differently. Here is what we find:

1. Peter contrasts verses 10-13 with the present heavens and earth, speaking of a thorough change that brings "new heavens and a new earth." The result of verses 10-13 is a completely different universe, one in which righteousness is thoroughly at home.

2. In verse 10 Peter speaks of the *stoicheia*, the basic elements of the earth. They will be "destroyed" (*luthēsetai*, from *luō*, a different word from that used in v. 7 [*apollumi*]). In fact this destruction comes by the process of burning up. This can in no way be interpreted as a renovation, as the author does (p. 131). Please note that the result (v. 13) is a different earth.

3. In verse 12 Peter uses the same word (*luō*) in reference to the heavens. The result is "a new heaven." In addition, here he says that the basic elements of the earth will melt through the heat of fire.

4. Associated with verse 10 is a difficult problem of textual criticism. One of the simplest solutions involves adopting the reading "will not be found" at the end of the verse. The end of the verse would then read (my translation),

> . . . and the earth and everything in it will not be found.

If this is valid, then the verse says that the present earth will disappear, and it would be impossible for the author to put this event during the seventieth week of Daniel and before the Millennium.

5. If the reading behind the Authorized Version is adopted, the result is the same: the (present) earth and everything in it will be burned up. The Authorized Version reads:

> . . . the earth also, and the works that are in it, shall be burned up.

The Time of the Introduction of the New Heavens and New Earth

The author argues that the new heavens and new earth of 2 Peter 3 refer to the period before the Millennium. There are several biblical details that argue against this.

First, Peter says (3:11-13) that believers during this age are to live godly lives in anticipation of the "day of God," which must be the same as the "day of the Lord" in verse 10. Taken as a whole, verses 1-13 teach that the believer, beset by sin now, looks forward to the absence of sin. In verse 13 Peter says that the new heavens and new earth will be the home of righteousness. While the Millennium will be a time of blessing, sin will still be present. Peter must be encouraging the believer to look beyond that time to a totally new earth.

The book of Revelation argues for this interpretation. In Revelation 21:1 John describes the new heaven and new earth. This is at a point after his description of the second coming of Christ (ch. 19), the Millennium (ch. 20), and the great white throne judgment (20:11-15).

He tells us that at that time no sin will be present (21:27) and that the throne of God and of the Lamb are present (22:3).

Conclusion

Peter's Day extends beyond the Kingdom, and the creation of the new heavens and new earth come after the Kingdom. We have seen in this chapter errors of fact, context, language, and logic.

<hr>

NOTES

1. For discussion of these and other logical fallacies, see, for example, David Kelley, *The Art of Reasoning* (New York: W. W. Norton and Company, 1988) and Howard Kahane, *Logic and Contemporary Rhetoric* (Belmont, CA: Wadsworth Publishing Company, 1988).

2. Graham Stanton, "Presuppositions in New Testament Criticism," in *New Testament Interpretation*, ed. I. Howard Marshall (Grand Rapids: Eerdmans, 1977), p. 68.

3. E. D. Hirsch, Jr., *Validity in Interpretation* (New Haven: Yale University Press, 1967), p. 165.

4. Hirsch, p. 167.

5. W. E. Vine, Merrill F. Unger, and William White, Jr. *An Expository Dictionary of Biblical Words* (Nashville: Thomas Nelson Publishers, 1985), p. x.

5

The Meaning and Length of "Great Tribulation"

T HE TRIBULATION has unique length and placement in the pre-wrath position—only the first part of the last half of the seventieth week of Daniel. In addition, it is "shortened" from a potential three-and-one-half year period. The author considers this to be an essential element of his position.

> The shortening of the Great Tribulation to less than three and one-half years is one of the most important truths to be grasped if the chronology of end-time events is to be understood. (p. 111)

How does the Bible speak of this period and its events?

Factual Errors

1. The Use of *Tribulation*

The author says,

> The designation *the tribulation period* should properly be omitted from any honest consideration of the time of the Rapture of the church. (p. 103)

He is correct in pointing out that it is biblically improper to speak of the seventieth week of Daniel as *the Tribulation period* (even though many do). But then he goes on to speak of the Great Tribulation, a phrase drawn from Revelation 7:14. We should observe carefully some biblical facts and distinctions. It is worth noting that the author asserts,

> Only six verses of Scripture can be clearly identified as using the word *tribulation* in a prophetic context. (p. 104)

Noting that one of the six is Deuteronomy 3:20, he discusses Matthew 24:21 and 29; Mark 13:19 and 24; and Revelation 7:14. However, he is factually incorrect. There are nine prophetically connected occurrences in the New Testament alone of the word commonly translated "tribulation" (*thlipsis*): Matthew 24:9, 21, and 29; Mark 13:19 and 24; Romans 2:9; and Revelation 2:9, 10, and 22, and 7:14. He does not mention Matthew 24:9, which occurs in the Olivet Discourse, and apparently does not consider the occurrences in Revelation 2 to be in a prophetic context (p. 104). Yet elsewhere in the book he says, concerning Revelation 2 and 3 (where the seven letters are found),

> How, then, should the letters to the seven churches be understood? Exactly as other prophetic truth is understood. (p. 288)

Furthermore, while here he says Revelation 2 is prophetic, in another place he tacitly assigns the passage to nonprophetic material.

Perhaps what he means is that only five New Testament occurrences describe global conditions associated with the seventieth week of Daniel. That we could agree with. But that is certainly not what he says on page 104.

2. The Use of *Great Tribulation*

The author says that the Great Tribulation is specifically referred to five times (Matt. 24:21, 29; Mark 13:19, 24; Rev. 7:14) (p. 107). He is factually incorrect here. The phrase *great tribulation* occurs in the Gospels only in Matthew 24:21.

The Shortening

It is crucial to the author's argumentation that the Great Tribulation be a definable period that is compressed from a possible three and one-half years to a shorter, undefined period of time. This allows him to have both the Great Tribulation and the Day of the Lord in the second half of the seven-year seventieth week.

The text of Matthew 24:22 reads,

> And except those days should be shortened, there should no flesh be saved; but for the elect's sake those days shall be shortened.

The author states,

> The entire seventieth week is not shortened . . . . What the Lord Himself teaches is shortened is the Great Tribulation. It is less than three and one-half years in duration. It begins in the middle of the seventieth week, but it does not run until the end of the seventieth week. (p. 109)

But there is a logical error here. We have no indication what the time period is shortened from and what it is shortened to. It is perfectly reasonable to assume that it might be shortened from ten years to seven, or from seven to three and one-half. In this the author has demonstrated the fallacy of the false dilemma again. The author has allowed only one choice—that the period is shortened from three and one-half years to a smaller duration. The Bible does not limit the reader to that one choice. Remember that the author considers this to be a key part of his argument for the pre-wrath Rapture, since he must have both the so-called Great Tribulation and then the Day of the Lord before the seventieth week is over.

He notes also that the timing of the seals, trumpets, and bowls hinges on this (p. 112). Thus, significant elements of his prophetic picture depend on the nature, duration and placement of the Great Tribulation. But once again, the author demonstrates factual, linguistic and logical errors. His case is certainly not what he makes it out to be.

No Practical Difference

It is noteworthy that the author does not show any practical difference between his Tribulation and the Day of the Lord; both are times of great difficulty on the earth. Yet he insists that the Day of the Lord is worse because it is the time of God's wrath. In terms of the Church and what it will or will not go through, there is no reason, based on the author's description of events, to say it will be bad for people in the Church during the Tribulation, but worse for people alive during the Day of the Lord, from which the Church is spared. This is also significant in relation to Israel. For example, the author says about his Tribulation period,

> [The Antichrist] will seek to become a world ruler, ruthlessly destroying men and nations as he moves to consolidate his power. His greatest fury will be unleashed against the Jewish nation. For that reason, this period of time is called "the time of Jacob's trouble." It will be a time of such severity that except those days were shortened, no flesh (in context, Jewish) would live. (p. 174)

What difference in suffering will there be for Israel between the Tribulation, which the author labels "the time of Jacob's trouble," and the Day of the Lord? Yet his whole position depends on seeing a crucial, practical distinction between the two periods.

Conclusion

The logical fallacy of the false dilemma is present in the author's attempt to show that the Great Tribulation will be shortened from three and one-half years. In addition, his Tribulation is not practically distinct from his Day of the Lord.

The Five Seals of Revelation 6

I N THE TIME SCHEME of the pre-wrath position, the seals of Revelation 6 occur before the Rapture and the Day of the Lord. While they involve difficulty for people on the earth, they are in no way the outpouring of the wrath of God, which does not come until the Day of the Lord. Is this what the text of Revelation really teaches? The answer is no.

The Theological Error

The author stresses that the events of the first five seals are based on the emergence of the Antichrist, represented by the white horse rider revealed by the first seal. He says that these five seals cannot be from God, since that would make God responsible for the Antichrist:

> If the seals are God's wrath, then God alone must take direct responsibility for a counterfeit religious system and the emergence of the Antichrist, for that is precisely what the first seal depicts. (p. 142)

This view of the seals demonstrates a faulty understanding of God's sovereignty. God is active in all the affairs of the universe, even in those that are sometimes described as involving His so-called permissive will. Weren't Satan's activities toward Job under God's control? Wasn't Babylon, as a persecutor of Israel, under God's control? The Old Testament actually describes God as raising up Babylon to discipline His people. Orthodox theologians have regularly stated that God controls human and angelic affairs but still cannot be charged with sin. It is theologically consistent for God to control the events of the first five seals and still not be chargeable with sin. Here, as elsewhere, God uses human beings and angels to bring about His purposes.

The Logical and Interpretive Errors

In Revelation 5 the Lamb, the Lord Jesus Christ in metaphor, seizes the scroll from the One who sits on the throne (God the Father), and in Revelation 6 He begins to open the seals contained in the scroll. The face-value interpretation of the seals is that they *contain* or *are* events that transpire on earth or events in the spiritual realm that touch on events on the earth.

However, not only does the author insist that the seals are not under Christ's control, since that would make Him responsible for events associated with the Antichrist, he also believes that the seals are not events and do not contain events. Instead, he says, the seals represent God's protective security over Christians during this time; God is protecting them until the Rapture. He argues that since *seal* in Ephesians 1:13 represents the security of the believer, as brought about by the Holy Spirit, so too in Revelation 6 the seals portray God's protection of the believer from any harm that God does not want to touch him.

Throughout the book the author appeals for the use of contextual, grammatical, historical, and literal interpretation. Here is the clearest example of his violating his avowed standards. It is exegetically indefensible to automatically transfer the meaning of a word in one text to a usage in another text without examining the context.

While seals in the Mediterranean world did have to do with security, we must ask how security is actually involved in Revelation 5 and 6. Many interpreters view the scroll as representing a will, a testament that reveals the disposing of the final events of the present world order. Seals were placed on wills, which took the form of a rolled scroll. A scroll could not be unrolled unless the seals were broken. This breaking plays a significant role in Revelation 5 and 6 and is described in the opening of each of the seven seals. In spiritual terms, the seals keep the seven parts of the scroll from being opened by anyone except the rightful Controller of events on the earth, the Lord Jesus Christ. This is the natural culturally and contextually based interpretation. Even if the scroll is not viewed as a will, it still must contain events. In addition, nowhere does chapter 6 indicate that the seals depict the well-being of believers. Yet the author asserts,

> The significance of the Lord Jesus Christ opening the seals is, among other things, the assurance of eternal security for those believers who may be martyred for Christ's sake. (p. 144)

Not only is this pure speculation, but it runs totally counter to the text of Revelation 5 and 6.

This way of dealing with the text is based on analogical reasoning, which, when done carefully, is a legitimate way of arguing a point. Analogical thinking proceeds on the basis of a comparison relationship between two or more entities and a prediction of an unknown or unspecified quality. For example, we can reason that since item A has qualities x, y, and z, and item B has qualities x and y, B must also have quality z, as item A does.

The accuracy of this kind of reasoning (that is, the strength of the analogy) depends on the strength and number of the correspondences. Number of correspondences without clear correspondence of known features counts for little. But strong positive correspondences, even in the absence of numbers, count for a great deal. Of course, negative correspondences weaken the analogy.

In arguing that the seals stand for the security of the believer, the author has on his side neither number of correspondences nor degree of positive correspondence between the seals of Ephesians 1:13 and of Revelation 6. The seal of Ephesians 1:13 is the Holy Spirit Himself and is explicitly described as a provision for keeping the believer secure in Christ. In Revelation 6 the seals are multiple, vary in their content, and are never associated with the work of the Holy Spirit. Most importantly, the seals themselves are "opened." As each seal is opened, something happens. Thus the seals *contain* or *are* events. Jesus opens them, thus demonstrating His control of the events. This breaking of the seals is precisely what the heavenly chorus praises Him for in 5:9.

The only correspondence between the use of *seal* in Ephesians 1 and in Revelation 5 and 6 is the element of security, which has quite different objects in the two passages: the believer versus events. If we are to follow sound principles of interpretation, we must assign consistent identification to the seals. They are events controlled by the Lord Jesus Christ and do not represent the security of the believer.

Unfortunately the type of interpretation (which might be described as "associative" exegesis) evidenced here by the author is finding its way more and more into evangelical handling of the Bible. It has no place in sound biblical scholarship.

Other Inconsistencies

1. According to the author's reasoning, if the seals are security and are opened or broken—which is what really happens—then the text would have to mean the opposite of what he wants it to mean. The broken seals would mean the believer is not kept secure.

2. Elsewhere the author asserts that the seventh seal contains the trumpet judgments and the bowls, which for him are events. Furthermore, if the seventh seal did represent security, then believers must be protected during the trumpets and bowls also. So the author splits the seventh seal off as being totally unlike the first six. For him it is a judgment (the wrath of God), but the first six seals are signs of security. There is no justification for this.

3. It is interesting that the author says,

> The Son, who is opening the seals, is in complete, sovereign control; nothing can happen to the child of God, even during the Great Tribulation, except that which his sovereign Lord permits. (p. 144)

As we noted above, he says that God is not responsible for the first six seals. Does he see God as sovereign or not? The author has displayed another contradiction between his statements.

Conclusion

Revelation 6 is another key passage for the pre-wrath view, since it is so involved with deciding on the starting point of the Day of the Lord (see p. 176). The author must keep the seals from coming directly from the hand of God and from containing any judgment from Him. His interpretation allows him to keep the seals from being of the same character as the trumpets and bowls, namely, judgments from God. But under a face-value interpretation of the seals, they are actually judgments unrolled as the scroll is opened. We should remind ourselves again of the author's own use of David Cooper's words:

> When the plain sense of Scripture makes common sense, seek no other sense . . . . (p. 176)

The author's theological misunderstanding and contextual and logical errors show that another of the crucial supports for his position is cracked beyond repair.

7

The Sixth Seal and
the Beginning of Wrath

S EVERAL Old and New Testament passages describe great changes
in the sun, moon, and stars in connection with the Day of the
Lord. In addition, Revelation 6:16 portrays people crying out for
mountains to bury them so they might escape from God's wrath. Are
these events directly connected, and do they signal the beginning of
the Day of the Lord?

This is a crucial area for the author, since it has to do with
determining when the Day of the Lord begins. He believes that the
sixth seal signals the starting point.

> The clear and repeated teaching of the Word of God is
> that there must be a cosmic disturbance of considerable
> magnitude before the Day of the Lord begins. (p. 148)

> But one must not allow the precision to go unnoticed.
> "The sun shall be turned into darkness, and the moon into
> blood, *before* the great and terrible day of the Lord come."
> Not only will there be cosmic disturbance, but it will
> occur before the Day of the Lord begins. (quoting Joel
> 2:31, p. 148)

The author is very concerned with chronological precision, but
apparently only when it suits his purposes. He takes the cosmic
disturbances of the sixth seal to be the same as those in the Day of the
Lord passages in the Old Testament. All well and good. However,
note that Joel 3:15, which follows the above-quoted passage by a few
verses, places the cosmic disturbances *after* the judgment of the
nations in 3:12.

The rocks of the sixth seal likewise come from the Old Testament, specifically Isaiah 2:21. The author must place these before the start of the Day of the Lord (p. 175). But an examination of Isaiah 2 discloses that these occur after the Day of the Lord has started. Either there are two occurrences (which he does not attempt to account for), his chronology is off, or a strict chronology is not possible at this point.

Furthermore, notice that Isaiah 2:10 and 21 speak of hiding under the rocks from the majesty of God. This strongly suggests the majestic presence of Christ and, thus, His glorious return to establish His Kingdom. But, as we will see in chapter 10, the author collapses the two advents without accounting for the tremendous differences in language between passages such as 1 Thessalonians 4, usually taken to be the Rapture, and Zechariah 14, usually taken to be the second advent. Thus, in the author's scheme Isaiah 2 would be putting the falling rocks after the beginning of the Day of the Lord. He has missed features of contexts and has forced his chronology.

The Sixth Seal and the Beginning of Wrath

1. Chronology

a. Wrath references

The author insists that the wrath passages in Revelation 8 through 16 are in "chronological sequence" (p. 172). However, the text of 11:15 and 17 describes Jesus as having begun to reign already. Here is verse 17b (my translation):

> . . . because you have taken your great power and have begun to reign.

In the pre-wrath position, then, Jesus is reigning in the Kingdom before the wrath is finished.

b. Wrath and the falling rocks

The author is inconsistent with himself concerning the relation of the falling rocks to the start of wrath. Here are Revelation 6:16 and 17:

> (16) And said to the mountains and rocks, Fall on us, and hide us from the face of him that sitteth on the throne, and from the wrath of the Lamb;
> (17) For the great day of his wrath is come, and who shall be able to stand?

The author asserts,

> It is clear that men flee from God's wrath after the sixth seal is opened. (p. 169)

> Only with the opening of the seventh seal and beyond is the word *wrath* mentioned in the book of Revelation. It can rightly be insisted, therefore, that the use of the word *wrath* is restricted to the events of the trumpets and bowls and, therefore, exempts the first six seals. (p. 171)

However, people are hiding because of wrath. Why would people hide from God, as described in the sixth seal, if the wrath were not yet present? He says,

> Even a cursory look at the Day of the Lord texts indicates that when God's Day of the Lord wrath begins, the world will know it. There will be no question about it. (p. 169)

If people will know when the wrath is present, they will also know when it is not present. He says the first trumpet comes as the content of the seventh seal and contains God's wrath. If God's wrath isn't present until the first trumpet, after the sixth seal, why are people hiding at the time of the sixth seal, especially if they can certainly tell the difference between the presence and absence of wrath?

Here is another example of inconsistency in the author's presentation. He claims that God's wrath does not start until the opening of the seventh seal (p. 172). But he demonstrates a contradiction by saying,

> After the opening of the sixth seal there is cosmic disturbance, and then men flee to the mountains to attempt to escape from God's wrath. (p. 170)

Indeed, people will know when the wrath is present, and they will hide to escape it. But when does the wrath actually begin? Hasn't it really started before this?

2. The aorist in Revelation 6:17

In order to keep wrath out of the time before the Day of the Lord, the author must also keep it out of the period of the first six seals. Some interpreters view the Greek word *ēlthen* in Revelation 6:17 (used with reference to the opening of the sixth seal) as placing wrath during the earlier seals. This word poses a problem for him, because it is a Greek verbal form that normally points to past time. However, the author asserts that *ēlthen* must refer to future time, to the period of the seventh seal, the first trumpet:

> Here then are two irrefutable parameters. In Revelation 6, with the opening of the sixth seal and the attendant cosmic disturbance, God's wrath "is come"—it is about to occur. (p. 180)

The author cannot simply have the verb refer to a present situation, since the wrath for him hasn't started yet. He must have it distinctly futuristic in order for it not to contradict his position. Is this linguistically justifiable? Is the futuristic character of *ēlthen* irrefutable? The author quotes several writers and summarizes their findings.

> All these men are clearly indicating that an aorist tense can be used to express either a past action or an event that is about to occur. (p. 165)

But the question that should be asked is, What does this particular verb mean *in its context*? If anything is true of Greek verbs, and particularly aorists, it is that the direction of time reference must be determined by usage in context. But the author never allows the context to speak. Instead, he keeps repeating his view that the wrath starts after the sixth seal. One of the first things that must be done in the interpretation of a particular Greek word is to look at nearby occurrences. In this case, we must ask how John uses the verb in the immediate surroundings, that is, in occurrences in the book of Revelation. John uses *ēlthen* of the arrival of events and people. Following are John's uses in the book of Revelation (other than 6:17) with reference to the arrival of events:

1. 11:18—thy wrath is come
2. 14:7—hour of his judgment is come
3. 14:15—the time is come for thee to reap

4. 18:10—in one hour is thy judgment come

5. 19:7—the marriage of the Lamb is come

The interpretation of any occurrence of *ēlthen* must take into account (1) the root meaning of the verb, (2) the aoristic component, and (3) the context. The normal way to interpret references 1, 2, 3, and 5 is that they refer to events that are present at the time of speaking. There is not necessarily a futuristic reference. The sense of the Greek word is that an event or condition has come on the scene, i.e., it is present at the time of speaking. The fourth reference, Revelation 18:10, *cannot possibly be futuristic*, since the preceding verse describes the judgment as present already.

In examining the occurrences of *ēlthen* in Revelation that involve the action of people (5:7; 7:13; 8:3; 17:1, 10; 21:9), we find that every one of them describes an event that occurs prior to the time of speaking. None is futuristic.

Here, then are several examples in the book of Revelation of past or present references using the verb *ēlthen*. Yet the author takes *ēlthen* in Revelation 6:17 as futuristic and rules out any possible past reference for it:

> . . . God's wrath "is come"—it is about to occur. (p. 180)

> As has been demonstrated, the aorist tense gives no basis
> for making that statement refer to a past event. (p. 167)

Up to the point of the second quote, he has demonstrated nothing about aorist verbs in the book of Revelation. Instead, he has just repeated his assertion that the aorist must be futuristic. He continues this insistence on a futuristic meaning by trying to show that wrath doesn't start until after the cosmic events and at the seventh seal. We have already shown the fallacy of these assertions. Thus, the author's logic is circular, and his solution for the aorist depends on arguments that are flawed in themselves.

In attempting to argue that *ēlthen* cannot look backward, the author asserts,

> There is no exegetical basis for making the sixth seal
> retroactive. The author consulted forty commentaries on
> the book of Revelation. Not one suggested that the sixth
> seal was retroactive and encompassed the events of the
> first five seals. (p. 167)

The issue is not whether the events of the sixth seal are retroactive, but whether or not the verb refers to something past, present, or future with respect to 6:17. The author's "irrefutable" parameter is based on a flawed linguistic foundation.

The Birth Pains

In attempting to show that wrath does not begin until the Day of the Lord, the author discusses the "birth pains" of Matthew 24:8 and 1 Thessalonians 5:2-3. Here are the two texts:

Matthew 24:8 (my translation)

All these are the beginning of birth pains.

1 Thessalonians 5:2-3

(2) For yourselves know perfectly that the day of the Lord so cometh as a thief in the night.
(3) For when they shall say, Peace and safety, then sudden destruction cometh upon them, as travail upon a woman with child, and they shall not escape.

In 1 Thessalonians 5:3, *travail* can be translated "labor pains." The author asserts that Matthew refers to the first half of the week, but Paul refers to the coming of the Day of the Lord. The first reference, according to him, is mild and just a beginning; the second is "hard labor" (p. 173). Apparently he does this to keep wrath (which he equates with "hard labor") out of the first half of the week,

However, both texts use the same Greek word—*ōdin*. If Matthew 24:8 is "labor," then so is 1 Thessalonians 5. The latter use cannot be construed to be speaking of a woman any further along in the birth process. In fact, Paul speaks of labor pains coming *on* a woman, *not* of her being in hard labor. The text reads (my translation),

Then sudden destruction will come on them as birth pains
on or *to* or *upon* a pregnant woman.

Matthew and Paul are talking about the same sudden and irreversible events. But once again the author believes he has an iron-clad case.

What becomes abundantly clear is this: The time immediately prior to the Day of the Lord is likened to a woman in travail (hard labor), but the first part of the seventieth week is likened to a woman with beginning birth pangs. (p. 173)

His linguistic error makes his assertion anything but "abundantly clear."

Peace and Safety

While arguing for the pre-wrath location of the seals, the author also asserts that people will cry "peace and safety" (1 Th. 5:3) just before the Day of the Lord (true) and also during his Tribulation period. This will be because of the activities of the Antichrist.

At the middle of the seventieth week the Antichrist will make his capital the city of Jerusalem (Dan.11:42-45). He will seek to become a world ruler, ruthlessly destroying men and nations as he moves to consolidate his power. His greatest fury will be unleashed against the Jewish nation. For that reason, this period of time is called "the time of Jacob's trouble." It will be a time of such severity that except those days were shortened, no flesh (in context, Jewish) would live. But for the elect's sake, those days will be shortened. At that moment cosmic disturbance will signal the approach of the Day of the Lord. Jews being persecuted by the Antichrist will view this as a divine intervention on their behalf in the nick of time. They will proclaim "peace and safety," but their cry will be premature—an expression of short-lived duration. (p. 174)

He goes on to say that the Day of the Lord will bring further trials for Israel. Note, incidentally, that the author splits the difficulties of the time of Jacob's trouble (for him, equated with a Tribulation period that starts at the middle of the seventieth week) and those of the Day of the Lord. He cannot, however, give any reason why Israel goes through two such periods of persecution. In any case, the question that must be asked here is, Why would Israel think that cosmic disturbances would signal divine intervention for them? There is nothing in any text of Scripture to suggest that Jews should think that such events would bring deliverance. In fact, in Luke 21 Jesus tells us how people will actually react.

> (25) And there shall be signs in the sun, and in the moon, and in the stars; and upon the earth distress of nations, with perplexity; the sea and the waves roaring;
> (26) Men's hearts failing them for fear, and for looking after those things which are coming on the earth; for the powers of heaven shall be shaken.
> (27) And then shall they see the Son of man coming in a cloud, with power and great glory.
> (28) And when these things begin to come to pass, then look up, and lift up your heads; for your redemption draweth near.

Jesus teaches that the heavenly signs are a direct prelude to the rescue of Israel at the time of His return for Israel's national redemption at the end of the seventieth week.

There is no justification anywhere in the Bible for the assertion that Israel would have reason to anticipate deliverance at the point where the author places the sixth seal, just before the Day of the Lord.

Silence in Heaven

In arguing that wrath doesn't begin until the Day of the Lord, the author also discusses Revelation 8:1, which precedes the sounding of the first trumpet:

> And when he had opened the seventh seal, there was silence in heaven about the space of half an hour.

He explains:

> Why this silence in heaven immediately prior to the trumpet judgments? Simply stated, because there is a command for silence associated with the outpouring of God's wrath during the Day of the Lord. In this regard,

the prophet Zephaniah wrote, "Hold thy peace at the presence of the Lord GOD; for the day of the LORD is at hand; for the LORD hath prepared a sacrifice, he hath bid his guests" (Zeph. 1:7). The world is called upon to be silent with the awareness that the Day of the Lord has arrived—that divine judgment is about to fall. (p. 171)

The author connects Zephaniah 1:7 and Revelation 8:1 to support his view that Revelation 8:1 anticipates the start of the Day of the Lord. This is the argument by analogy again, as we saw with the seals and Ephesians 1. His reasoning goes this way: Zephaniah has silence, and it refers to the Day of the Lord; Revelation 8:1 has silence; the two silences must be the same; therefore, Revelation 8:1 anticipates the Day of the Lord. So at the end of his chapter 12 he asserts,

The Bible says there is silence in heaven at the start of the Day of the Lord (Zeph. 1:7). Silence is said to occur with the opening of the seventh seal (Rev. 8:1). (p. 176)

He thus takes the two passages as referring to the same event.

The facts do not support him here. There is a difference between the two passages. In context, Zephaniah 1:7 is telling human beings *on earth* to be silent. John says the silence is *in heaven*. Heaven and earth are not the same! Heavenly citizens and earthly citizens are not the same!

Conclusion

The author's placement of cosmic disturbances with respect to the beginning of the wrath of the Day of the Lord is not consonant with the text of Revelation 6. His treatments of *ēlthen* and *ōdin*, and his reasoning concerning "peace and safety" and the silence in heaven are seriously flawed. All of this argues against his assertions concerning the beginning point of the Day of the Lord.

8

Events at the Time of the Pre-Wrath Rapture

T HE SEVENTIETH WEEK OF DANIEL will contain a wide variety of events, individuals, and world movements. Sorting them out is a difficult task. The author associates many of them with his Rapture of the Church. How accurate is he?

The Trumpets

1. Collapsing

The author tries to equate the last trumpet of 1 Corinthians 15:52, the trumpet call of God of 1 Thessalonians 4:16, the trumpet of Joel 2:1, and the trumpets of Revelation 8:7ff. A careful examination of the biblical text will show that only two of these refer to the same event—1 Corinthians 15:52 and 1 Thessalonians 4:16.

a. The first two passages speak of events that occur when believers of this age are taken to be with God. Both describe (1) resurrection of believers physically dead at the time and (2) the change in living believers. Both also describe the Rapture. The trumpet in 1 Thessalonians 4:16 is called "God's trumpet." Both trumpets sound for gathering in anticipation of a positive event. In 1 Thessalonians 4:16 the anticipated event is meeting Christ *in the air*.

b. On the other hand, Joel 2:1 is a command given to human beings to blow a warning trumpet, to sound in Israel an alarm warning of impending danger, of preparation for war.

c. In Revelation 8:7ff. the trumpets contain events that are judgments. They are sounded by angels and have no hope connected with them. The first six are fire and blood, the sea turned to blood, poisoning of water, changes in the heavens, demonic oppression, and the army from the east. Revelation 9:20 tells us that these are "plagues" or "blows." The seventh trumpet (11:15-19), which has no content like the others, brings the action up to the Kingdom. Many premillennial interpreters of Revelation believe that the seven bowl judgments constitute the seventh trumpet. This is based partly on (1) the lack of content for the seventh trumpet that is similar to the others and (2) the statements of 8:13 and 11:14, which appear to describe trumpets five, six, and seven as three last woes. The woe of the seventh trumpet would then be the seven bowls.

d. In Rev. 8:7ff. there are seven distinct trumpets, not just one. While they are a series, the book of Revelation never refers to them as "one trumpet." They each have their own identity. Yet the author claims they are one trumpet.

> As the seventh seal is opened, the seven trumpet and bowl judgments progressively unfold. They are part of a comprehensive whole. Collectively, they are God's Day of the Lord wrath, His final eschatological judgment—the last trump. (p. 193)

Elsewhere he stresses distinctions between singular and plural. Yet here he makes a plural singular in order to make the "trumpets" fit the last "trumpet." Here is a biblical fact: 1 Corinthians 15:52 does not say "at the last seven trumpets" or even "at the last trumpets"! If the author were really consistent with his own attempt to make the Rapture fit with the trumpets of Revelation, he would have to say that the Rapture would have to occur at the last of the seven trumpets, which is the bowls. Of course, this is much too late for him, though. Nevertheless he claims,

> The Rapture must occur at the opening of the seventh seal and immediately prior to the beginning of God's wrath. That interpretation is unstrained and biblically accurate. (p. 194)

It is "unstrained" only if one ignores biblical distinctions. A simple chart of features will help us to visualize the distinctions.

	Trumpeter	Purpose	Result
1 Corinthians 15	Not Stated	Gather	Resurrection
1 Thessalonians 4	God	Gather in Air	Resurrection and Rapture
Joel 2	Humans	Assemble and Warn of Danger	War and Invasion
Revelation 8ff.	Angels	Bring Events	Judgments

The first two passages are very much alike, and Joel 2 and Revelation 8ff. are different and distinctive. Yet in spite of all these differences, the author collapses them. Furthermore, if the trumpets of Revelation 8ff. describe the Rapture and the beginning of the Day of the Lord, why is no Rapture mentioned there? There is only judgment!

Since the author seems to want to equate all eschatological trumpets, it is worth noting Zechariah 9:14, where the Lord Jesus Christ blows a trumpet on the day of His appearance. Its purpose is to announce His presence as a warrior who has come to rescue Israel. "On that day" (v. 16) he will save Israel. This must be at His second coming at the end of Daniel's seventieth week. Not all eschatological trumpets are alike!

2. The Contents of the Fourth Trumpet

It is significant that the fourth trumpet (8:12) *contains* or *is* cosmic disturbances parallel to those of the sixth seal (6:12-14). Many interpreters have noted that exactly the same objects are affected in each: the sun, the moon, and the stars. Many interpreters take the fourth trumpet to be an augmentation of the sixth seal. However, remember that the author insists that cosmic disturbances are a sign preceding the Day of the Lord. Yet this trumpet would, for him, have to be well into the Day of the Lord. He has apparently failed to note this inconsistency. Don't forget, he says we must be careful with the text of the Bible.

3. Involvement of Angels

The author asserts many times that the seals are not from God's hand but are Satan and Antichrist's activities. God would not be responsible for foisting their work on the earth. In addition, angels are not mentioned in connection with the seals, he says, because they do God's bidding, not Satan's. Thus, he says,

> Again, the first five seals represent the ultimate rebellion of man under the Antichrist, who is empowered by Satan. Thus, no angelic beings were involved. (p. 181)

But notice the the fifth trumpet. It causes the release of tormenters having one named Abbadon or Apollyon as their king (9:11). Both terms mean "destroyer." He is a star fallen from heaven (9:1) and controls the abyss. The tormenters perpetrate affliction that matches what we see elsewhere in the Bible as demonic oppression. All the features of Revelation 9:1-11 point to the conclusion of many premillennial interpreters: the leader is Satan. If this is so, then please note that an angel of God blows the fifth trumpet with the result that Satan releases demons to torture human beings. Yet this runs directly counter to his repeated assertion that God's (unfallen) angels do not support Satan's activity.

The Groups of Revelation 7

1. The 144,000

In reference to Revelation 7:2-3, in which angels are told not to harm the land or the sea or the trees until a seal is put on the foreheads of the servants of our God, the author says,

> The message is clear, urgent, precise, and given as a command: Do not begin pouring out God's wrath until the remnant of 144,000 Jews are first sealed for protection from that wrath. (p. 181)

The Bible does not say at this point that the wrath is beginning. Yet he says that such content is clear and precise. This is based, once again, on his assumption that the wrath begins precisely at his time for the Rapture and start of the Day of the Lord. Clarity and precision must have the support of the facts.

2. The Multitude: The True Church?

The author boldly states that the multitude of Revelation 7 is the "true church" (p. 185). He provides no support for this from the Bible. The text of Scripture says no such thing! Remember that elsewhere, many times, he says that if *wrath* isn't used in chapter 6, then the events are not God's wrath. Let's turn the tables: If there's no use of *Church*, we cannot take this as the Church! Furthermore, there is no support for his statement that they are raptured at the end of the Great Tribulation but before the Day of the Lord begins. Again, the Bible does not say this. This can be accepted only if many broken links in a complicated chain are accepted.

Noah and the Flood

The author attempts to counter any suggestion that the Day of the Lord begins some time after the Rapture. Some dispensationalists have posited this time gap in order to account for the appearance of Elijah (Mal. 4:5) and the manifestation of the Antichrist (p. 159). The author maintains that the Rapture, the start of the wrath of God and the beginning of Day of the Lord all come at the same time—after the middle of the seventieth week of Daniel and after the Tribulation period. One of the main supports he uses for this is Jesus' mentioning of Noah in Matthew 24:37-39 in connection with His second coming. Following is the text of that passage:

> (36) But of that day and hour knoweth no man, no, not the angels of heaven, but my Father only.
> (37) But as the days of Noah were, so shall also the coming of the Son of man be.
> (38) For as in the days that were before the flood they were eating and drinking, marrying and giving in mar-

riage, until the day that Noah entered into the ark,
(39) And knew not until the flood came, and took them all away, so shall also the coming of the Son of man be.

The author states,

> The Lord teaches that on the very day that Noah entered the ark, God's judgment fell. In other words, there was deliverance for Noah and his family and judgment on the unregenerate world on the same day. Then the Lord makes this point: "But as the days of Noah were, so shall also the coming of the Son of man be." That is, deliverance of the righteous will be immediately followed by God's Day of the Lord wrath on the wicked. *Biblically, no extended period of time can separate the two events of rapture and wrath.* (p. 196)

But is this Jesus' point? Remember, He is using an analogy, and analogies can never be pressed to yield correspondence in every detail. Why does Jesus use the events of Noah's day to illustrate His coming? He gives the answer Himself in Matthew 24:40-42. There will be sudden judgment, so people should be watchful. That is Jesus' point as based on the Noah account.

There are many features of the Noah account that are potentially eligible as contributing to Jesus' point regarding His coming. But the author only picks the "same day" feature. Why not assert that there will be a flood at the time of the Rapture? Or the loss of life of all but eight people? Again, he has picked what he wants to use to support his position. In this case, he has even missed the main point of Jesus' comparison.

It is worth noting at this point that the context of the "coming" in Matthew 24:39 is a glorious return (Mt. 24:30; 25:31). The author uses this passage in reference to the Rapture of the Church, something that the Bible describes in very different terms. We will deal with this at length in chapter 11.

In a later discussion of the Noah account, the author writes,

> As the flood began on the same day as Noah entered the ark, so the Lord taught that the Rapture would occur on the same day as the Day of the Lord begins (Lk. 17:26-27, 30). (p. 220)

It should be obvious by now that Jesus "taught" no such thing. He used Noah's time to teach that His second coming would be unexpected.

But there is something in the Bible that makes this argument even more fallacious. Consider the text of Genesis 7:1-10.

> (1) And the LORD said unto Noah, Come thou and all thy house into the ark; for thee have I seen righteous before me in this generation.
> (2) Of every clean beast thou shalt take to thee by sevens, the male and his female; and of beasts that are not clean by two, the male and his female.
> (3) Of fowls also of the air by sevens, the male and the female, to keep seed alive upon the face of all the earth.
> (4) For yet seven days, and I will cause it to rain upon the earth forty days and forty nights; and every living thing that I have made will I destroy from off the face of the earth.
> (5) And Noah did according unto all that the LORD commanded him.
> (6) And Noah was six hundred years old when the flood of waters was upon the earth.
> (7) And Noah went in, and his sons, and his wife, and his sons' wives with him, into the ark, because of the waters of the flood.
> (8) Of clean beasts, and of beasts that are not clean, and of fowls, and of every thing that creepeth upon the earth,
> (9) There went in two and two unto Noah into the ark, the male and the female, as God had commanded Noah.
> (10) And it came to pass after seven days, that the waters of the flood were upon the earth.

Did you notice when Noah entered the ark and when the floods came? The two events were seven days apart. The author claims that they occurred on the same day! Look carefully also at Matthew 24:38-39, where Jesus says that people kept on eating and drinking until the day Noah entered the ark. It does not say that the flood came the day Noah entered. Recall that the author says,

> Scripture has been cited to demonstrate that the Rapture and the Day of the Lord are intimately connected, and no

significant period of time between these two events can possibly be established. (p. 159)

The account of Noah provides him no support at all for this.

The "Apostasy"

1. The Participants

Paul teaches that the start of the Day of the Lord cannot take place until the "falling away" or "rebellion" occurs (the Greek word is *apostasia*, 2 Th. 2:3). The author correctly notes that Luke uses the same Greek word in Acts 21:2 in reference to Jews who were complaining that Paul had told them to "turn away from" Moses, i.e., the Law. But then he states,

> When Paul used the word *apostasy* in 2 Thessalonians 2:3,
> he did so in exactly the same way as Dr. Luke. He was
> speaking of Jews who, during the seventieth week of
> Daniel, will totally abandon the God of their fathers and
> their messianic hope in favor of a . . . false messiah . . . .
> (p. 198)

Luke *could* be using it the same way, but there is absolutely no support in the text of Acts for this assertion. Yet the author goes on to make this assumption the basis for further argumentation.

> This view is in marked contrast with the general view of
> pretribulation rapturism. The usual position is that Paul
> was speaking of believers in this age who will apostatize
> before the Rapture and the beginning of the seventieth
> week. (p. 198)

He then argues for several pages that Israel is alone in this "apostasy," relating it to the apostasy of the second century B.C. in the days of Antiochus Epiphanes and describing parallels between that ruler and the "Antichrist."

> In that future day, the apostasizing Jews will believe that
> the covenant they are making will bring them protection
> from the surrounding nations. That is precisely what such

> Jews thought when they made a covenant with Antiochus Epiphanes. In reality, it will be a covenant with death. (p. 205)

As elsewhere, he makes an assumption, says it over and over so that it appears to be an established fact, then uses it in argumentation as if it is established. As he continues to argue this point, he claims the following:

> The apostasy, to which Paul referred (2 Th. 2:3-4), will involve Israel, not the church. It will commence when many within the nation sign a covenant with the Antichrist (unknown to them, a covenant with death) at the beginning of that seventieth week. The apostasy will encompass a total *abandonment* or *falling away* from renewed covenant relationship . . . . (p. 206)

As to this abandonment of "renewed covenant relationship," please note that the author gives no support whatever for this, and he cannot, because the Bible never says this. It is pure conjecture on his part.

It appears that the author identifies the "apostasy" as he does in order to have it come before the Day of the Lord begins and the man of sin is revealed in the middle of the seventieth week (p. 207), and to have the apostasy inside the seventieth week, not before it begins (p. 207).

2. The Language

The author asserts that the word *apostasia* has the definite article in front of it and thus refers to "a specific, definitive, identifiable event, not some kind of nebulous apostasy at the end of this age" (p. 199). However, it is not linguistically valid to say that the presence of a definite article in front of a Greek noun makes that noun refer to one particular occasion. In ancient Greek, abstract nouns such as *apostasia* varied in their use of the article with no difference in meaning.[1] A good example of this is Ephesians 2, where verses 5 and 8 have the noun *charis* ("grace") without and with the article, respectively, with no apparent difference in meaning. More importantly, even if an identifiable event were in view in 2 Thessalonians 2, the author would have to show that this is a particular Jewish apostasy.

Elijah

The author argues that Elijah is one of the two witnesses of Revelation 11:3 and that his ministry will coincide with the last half of the seventieth week (pp. 160-61). His charts show the coming of Elijah at the beginning of the Day of the Lord and at the time of the Rapture (p. 161). He notes that Malachi 4:5 predicts that Elijah will come before the Day of the Lord. He concludes,

> Elijah is seen to be ministering inside and during the seventieth week. (p. 157)

and

> Elijah (or one like him) is to minister for precisely three and one-half years, which almost certainly relates to one-half of the seventieth week (Rev. 11:3). (p. 159)

However, this is based on the assumption that he is one of the two witnesses within the seventieth week. Revelation 11 never says that he is. And even if he were one of the witnesses, does the author's timing work? The author asserts that the book of Revelation is sequential. Describing his book as a whole, he asserts,

> A by-product of the view herein espoused is a clear, logical, and sequential interpretation of the book of Revelation . . . . (p. 85)

Why then does this individual not appear until Revelation 11, since in the author's scheme he is supposed to appear before the Day of the Lord? Revelation 11:3 places the ministry of the two witnesses *between the sixth and seventh trumpets.* This is *after* the author's Rapture and his start of the Day of the Lord, yet he insists that Elijah appears *before* the Rapture and *before* the first trumpet. Either Revelation is not as sequential as he thinks it is (but remember—much of his position depends on this), or Elijah doesn't come where he says he does.

Conclusion

The pre-wrath view of the "last trump" fails to notice distinctions among biblical trumpets. Its treatment of the 144,000 is based on earlier errors and argues from nonexistent data. There are evident linguistic mistakes in its view of the "apostasy" in 2 Thessalonians 2. But most glaring of all is the factual error concerning Noah and his entry point into the ark in relation to the start of the flood.

NOTES

1. Nigel Turner, *A Grammar of New Testament Greek*, vol. 3 of *A Grammar of New Testament Greek*, by James Hope Moulton (Edinburgh: T. & T. Clark, 1963), p. 176.

9

The Beast

THE BIBLE teaches that a powerful and particularly evil world ruler will emerge in connection with the Day of the Lord and the seventieth week of Daniel. He is referred to in various ways in the Bible, in order to highlight the various facets of his character and activity. The author makes some startling claims about him. Do they fit with the Bible?

The author asserts that Revelation 17:11 teaches this world ruler is resurrected.

> John has still more to say concerning this coming Antichrist: "And the beast that was, and is not, even he is the eighth, and is of the seven . . . and goeth into perdition" (Rev. 17:11). Once again, the strong implication of the text is that the Antichrist once lived and ruled over a nation, then died, and will be raised to rule over the eighth empire. This should not be surprising. Since the Antichrist will be a counterfeit Christ, he will also perform a counterfeit resurrection. He . . . will be raised, but he will die again and go "into perdition." Jesus was not simply raised; He was resurrected, never to die again. (p. 209)

There are significant theological implications in this assertion. First, the author makes a distinction between resurrection and raising from the dead. Resurrection, he says, means more than raising from the dead; it means one never dies again. However, according to the Bible, any bringing back to life of a dead person is a resurrection. There are two main words or word groups that are used of raising the dead in the New Testament: (1) the verb *anistēmi*, "to raise," and the noun *anastasis*, "raising," and (2) the verb *egeirō*, "to raise." Both are used of

71

Jesus and others who were brought back to life. Here are some examples:

Hebrews 11:35, using *anastasis*:

Women received their dead raised to life again . . . .

This is the same word that is used throughout the New Testament to refer to Christ's resurrection.

Matthew 27:52, using *egeirō*:

And the graves were opened; and many bodies of the saints that slept were raised.

John 12:1, using *egeirō*:

Then Jesus, six days before the passover, came to Bethany, where Lazarus was, who had been dead, whom he raised from the dead.

Would the author assert that these people didn't die again? See also Matthew 17:9; 27:64; John 2:22; and Acts 3:15 for other uses of *egeirō* to refer to resurrection in general.

Both *egeirō* and *anistēmi/anastasis* describe the same thing for Jesus and others—being brought back to physical life after physical death. It is biblically impossible to make a distinction between resurrection and raising from the dead. Yes, it is true that Jesus never faced death again, but that is a feature that is in addition to His being resurrected. In fact, Paul asserts this in Acts 13:34, where he says that Jesus' resurrection also contained a promise of never dying again, as predicted in Isaiah 55:3 and Psalm 16:10. Here, then, are theological and linguistic errors on the author's part.

But there is an even more striking theological problem here. The author is asserting that the Antichrist is raised from the dead. Is this possible?

First, a careful examination of the text will disclose that it does not really say that the beast dies. Revelation 13:1-3 teaches that the beast out of the sea will have ten horns and seven heads, with ten crowns on his horns. At times the beast is described as an individual, at times as an empire. The beast is an empire in that the beast as a whole has seven heads. Revelation 17:10-11 explains that the beast consists of seven kings plus one. That they are sequential is indicated by 17:10.

The eighth beast is the epitome of all that preceded and so receives the same name as the group. Revelation 17:11 says that he belongs to the seven. It is one of the earlier kings that is wounded, not the individual who is the eighth king. To put it another way, the beast coming out of the sea has seven heads, and one is wounded before the beast comes on the scene. Revelation 13:3 is quite careful about this (my translation):

> And one of his heads seemed to have had a fatal wound....

What the wound is, who receives it, and how it is healed is simply not stated.

The author is unclear as to who he believes does the raising. At one point he says the Antichrist will "perform a counterfeit resurrection" (p. 209). Yet he speaks of the beast as being "raised" (p. 209) and also says that the Antichrist will be directly energized by Satan (p. 210). Is he claiming that a human being has the power to raise himself? Or is he claiming indirectly that Satan has the power to do the raising? Either way, there are serious theological problems.

It is questionable whether Satan has the power to restore to life one who has died, even though his power is great. The Bible never says that an individual is brought back to life by someone other than God. It appears that the Bible teaches that only God has power to raise people from the dead. This is the distinct province of Jehovah throughout the Old and New Testaments. In fact, Romans 4 describes Him as unique because of this capacity: He is the God who gives life to the dead.

There are some who interpret Revelation 13 as teaching that God raises the Antichrist. Even under this interpretation, the Antichrist would not be raised by Satan, nor would he raise himself. Some commentators have been careless with the details of this passage and the theological implications of claiming that an individual is genuinely raised from the dead by someone other than the God of the Bible.

10

The Restrainer

I N 2 THESSALONIANS 2 Paul indicates that the Day of the Lord cannot begin until a "restrainer" is first removed. For centuries the identity and work of that restrainer have been debated. The author makes some unusual claims about the restrainer, the object of the restraining, and the timing of the restraint and its cessation. Are they accurate?

Following are some of the things he says concerning the restrainer:

> The one who had the job of hindering the Antichrist will step aside; that is, he will no longer be a restraint between the Antichrist and those the Antichrist is persecuting.
> . . . The Bible is explicit that the archangel Michael is the personage who will *step aside.* (p. 257)

> The Word of God teaches that the restrainer is the archangel Michael . . . . (p. 260)

In addition, he asserts,

> The hinderer . . . is not removed before the Day of the Lord. He is removed in the middle of the seventieth week with the occurrence of the abomination that makes the temple desolate. (p. 256)

> Michael will no longer hinder or hold down the wicked one; he will *step aside;* that is, from between Israel and Satan. (p. 260)

> Michael, Israel's great prince, shall stand up . . . from helping Israel during the time of the Great Tribulation (v. 1a). (p. 267)

The word *hindereth* means *to hold down,* and the phrase *taken out of the way* means *to step aside.* (p. 257)

Here is what the author claims:

1. The restrainer is Michael. The Bible is explicit in this identification.
2. Restraining means holding back the Antichrist in his persecution of Israel.
3. Restraining means holding back Satan.
4. Restraining means helping Israel.
5. Michael stands up and also steps aside from helping Israel.
6. *Taken out of the way* in 2 Thessalonians 2 means "step aside."
7. *Hinder* means "hold down."

But what does the Bible actually say? Is it "explicit" in these things, as the author claims?

The Work of Restraining

Here is the text of 2 Thessalonians 2:5-8:

(5) Remember ye not that, when I was yet with you, I told you these things?

(6) And now ye know what restraineth that he might be revealed in his time.

(7) For the mystery of iniquity doth already work; only he who now hindereth will continue to hinder until he be taken out of the way.

(8) And then shall that wicked one be revealed, whom the Lord shall consume with the spirit of his mouth, and shall destroy with the brightness of his coming,

Note the following features in this passage and their implications for the identification of the restrainer:

1. In verse 6 Paul identifies the restraining work as preventing the lawless one from being publicly recognized. When the restraint ceases at the appropriate time, revelation occurs. Verses 7 and 8 have the same feature: When the restrainer is removed, the lawless one will be revealed. It does not say the restraining work is directed at Satan. It

does not say the restraining work involves holding back the Antichrist in his persecution of Israel. It does not say the restraining means protecting Israel.

A careful examination of the Greek text shows that the hindering is never said to be directed at the lawless one's activity, his "lawlessness," per se. Instead, it is directed at "the mystery of iniquity." Apparently this must reach a peak before the "man of sin" can arise and begin his work. The text of 7b reads (my translation),

> but the one who now holds back (or "is holding back")
> will continue to do so.

The restraining thus has as its object the "mystery of iniquity" and the disclosure of the lawless one, not his activity. The author is correct in pointing out that *hinder* means "hold down." The lawless one is kept from public manifestation.

2. The Greek text of 2 Thessalonians 2:7 says literally that the restrainer "comes to be out of the middle," i.e., his position changes from being in the middle (his place of restraining) to being somewhere else. He does not "step aside." There is no legitimate way that the Greek text by itself can be translated "step aside." It simply does not say that.

3. The restraining was going on in Paul's day and during every generation since 2 Thessalonians was written ("is holding back"). If the Antichrist is a person, he could not have been alive at that time. However, the author asserts that the restraining work was directed at persecution of Israel by the Antichrist. Why was there a restraining work when he wasn't alive? This is another reason why it is best to take the hindering as referring to the power of lawlessness and not to the Antichrist.

The Identity of the Restrainer

This is a crucial point for the author, since under his system he must account for the removal of the restrainer; but, wanting to keep the Church present throughout the period, he must also have the Holy Spirit present. Thus, his system automatically rules out the Holy Spirit as the restrainer (many interpreters hold that He is the restrainer, as suggested in part by Gen. 6:3), and Michael gets the job of abandoning Israel. Aside from the fact that no reason is given in Scripture for such an act (i.e., why protection would stop), there are serious linguistic problems with this.

The author asserts that the Hebrew verb *'amad* found in Dan. 12:1 can mean "stand still" (p. 258). In some of its occurrences in the Old Testament it does. But the author goes further and says that "stand still" means "stand aside," i.e., act passively and allow something to happen. Please note these details:

1. According to Brown, Driver, and Briggs' lexicon, the standard scholarly Hebrew lexicon, *'amad* never means "stand aside."[1]

2. "Stand still" and "stand aside" are not the same thing. Allow me to give an example. If I am taking a picture of my children and one wiggles, I might say, "Stand still." But if I say, "Stand aside," my child would move out of the picture. These are two different verbs and two different actions!

3. The author cites one Hebrew scholar who gives the meaning of *'amad* as "stand still." Citing one commentator for the meaning of a word is hardly convincing. What do the others say? What are the possible meanings for the word? Furthermore, the author changes the commentator's conclusion.

> The meaning, according to one of Israel's greatest scholars, would be to *stand aside* or *be inactive*. (p. 258)

The commentator only said it meant "stand still." Again, "stand still" and "stand aside" are not the same thing.

4. According to my count, the verb *'amad* occurs 30 times in Daniel. In none of its occurrences does it mean "stand still passively to allow something to happen." In fact, in the latter chapters, when a new personage is introduced to the narrative, the verb is often used as equivalent to our "come on the scene."

5. The author might argue that in some of its occurrences the verb means "turn away from." That won't work, either, because in those instances in the Old Testament it is found with the Hebrew preposition equivalent to our word *from*, giving the idea of "standing away from." Moreover, this is still not the same thing as "allowing something to happen."

6. The face-value interpretation of Daniel 12:1 makes a connection between the standing of Michael in 1a and the deliverance of Daniel's people in 1c. Michael stands up to save Israel. His standing and the deliverance both occur "at that time." The emphasis of the verse is on protection, not abandonment.

7. The author cites two occurrences in Job and Nehemiah where 'amad means "stand still." Here is Job 32:16:

> When I had waited (for they spoke not, but stood still, and answered no more),

The author interprets this to mean they "kept quiet" or "desisted" (p. 258). They may have been quiet and standing still, but the information on the desisting is found in the statements about their silence and lack of reply, not in the word 'amad. Here is Nehemiah 8:5:

> And Ezra opened the book in the sight of all the people (for he was above all the people); and when he opened it, all the people stood up.

The author says that here 'amad means the people "desisted" (p. 258). They may have kept quiet, but 'amad doesn't carry that information. It is implied by their standing respectfully and listening to Ezra read the law. Again, standing still isn't the same thing as desisting or standing aside. Nehemiah 8:5 does not say "and as he opened it the people stood aside or were inactive"!

The author's treatment of both passages demonstrates the logical fallacy of *false cause*. Here is an example of this. A person arrives at a bus stop and immediately a bus comes. The individual concludes that the bus came because he came, ignoring the fact that the bus was simply keeping its schedule. In a similar fashion, the author has attributed to 'amad the information that is conveyed by other portions of sentences.

8. The author's rendering of 'amad would lead to a logical contradiction in Daniel 12:1, which uses the verb twice. His interpretation would make the verse read in a very strange way, because it would contain a redundancy.

> Michael, the great prince who stands aside for your people, will stand aside.

Conclusions

Here is what we can confirm concerning 2 Thessalonians 2 and Daniel 12:

1. The Bible nowhere describes Michael as stepping aside so that God's wrath can fall on Israel. In addition, it never says that anyone or anything steps aside or is removed in order that God's wrath can be manifested.

2. The author describes Michael's stepping aside as a clear fact (p. 259). Simply saying over and over that something is a fact doesn't make it so. Does the text of Scripture actually support the assertion or not? In this case, the linguistic and textual evidence proves the assertion false.

3. The author states,

> It is clear that the restrainer is neither human government nor the blessed Holy Spirit of God. The Word of God teaches that the restrainer is the archangel Michael . . . . (p. 260)

A careful treatment of Daniel 12:1 and *'amad* shows that not only is this not clear, it is incorrect.

4. In connecting Daniel 12:1 and 2 Thessalonians 2, the author claims,

> Michael will no longer hinder or hold down the wicked one; he will *step aside*; that is, from between Israel and Satan. (p. 260)

The Bible never says this. The restraining of 2 Thessalonians 2 is directed at the "mystery of iniquity."

5. In regard to Michael's supposed work, he says,

> All of this activity fits, unstrained and perfectly, into a prewrath rapture of the church. (p. 260)

It can be unstrained and have a perfect fit only if one ignores the facts of the Bible.

Many years ago a competent commentator on the New Testament, speaking of certain approaches to Revelation 20, pointedly described the kind of biblical interpretation that takes such liberties with the text, saying it means that,

> there is an end of all significance in language, and Scripture is wiped out as a definite testimony to any thing.[2]

NOTES

1. Francis Brown, S. R. Driver, and Charles A. Briggs, *A Hebrew and English Lexicon of the Old Testament* (Oxford: Oxford University Press, 1962), pp. 763-65.

2. Henry Alford, *The Greek Testament*, 4 vols. (London: Longmans, Green, 1894), vol. 4, pp. 732-33.

11

The Coming of Christ

P REMILLENNIALISTS—people who hold that Christ will rule visibly on the earth—hold that the Bible describes a coming of Christ to receive His Church and a coming in glory after that. The amount of time that falls between these comings has been debated. However, the author of *The Pre-Wrath Rapture* does something unusual with these two events: he collapses them, asserting that Christ (1) takes His Church from the earth before the Day of the Lord, (2) remains on the scene, and (3) gloriously judges the nations and establishes His Kingdom. Is this true?

The Meaning of *Parousia*

1. The Author's Assertion

For the author, the word *parousia* is a key term to describe Christ's return. In the pre-wrath view, Christ comes and then has "a continuous presence for the purpose of rapturing the Church and judging the wicked" (p. 217). In addition, it holds that "His second coming will include the Rapture of the Church, the Day of the Lord judgment, and His return in glory (p. 218).

The author points out that the Greek word *parousia* is used of events corresponding to the Rapture of the Church (e.g., 1 Th. 4:15) and to His "second advent" (e.g., Mt. 24:3). That is true. But he also asserts that the word "means a coming and continuing presence" (p. 222). There are two questions that must be dealt with: (1) Does *parousia* mean coming and presence? and (2) Does *parousia* support the author's contention that Christ comes and stays continuously, or are there two separate comings? We must ask of the text, then, Are both arrival and presence always indicated by New Testament usage?

2. *Parousia* as "Presence" Only

The word *parousia* can mean "arrival" or "coming" as the prelude to a presence. And it can also refer to the presence itself. The author correctly cites 2 Corinthians 10:10 and Philippians 2:12 as describing Paul's presence. However, notice that there is no element of coming in these. The emphasis is all on the presence in these passages. Here is 2 Corinthians 10:10:

> For his letters, say they, are weighty and powerful, but his bodily presence [*parousia*] is weak, and his speech contemptible.

Now let's substitute what the author thinks *parousia* means.

> For his letters, say they, are weighty and powerful, but his arrival and presence are weak, and his speech contemptible.

And here is Philippians 2:12:

> Wherefore, my beloved, as ye have always obeyed, not as in my presence only but now much more in my absence, work out your own salvation with fear and trembling.

Again, let's substitute what the author thinks *parousia* means:

> Wherefore, my beloved, as ye have always obeyed, not as in my arrival and presence only but now much more in my absence, work out your own salvation with fear and trembling.

In both cases, seeing an element of arrival leads to nonsense. Yet that is what the author would have us do with *parousia*.

3. *Parousia* as "Coming" Only

There are a number of occurrences of *parousia* in the New Testament where there is no element of "presence" in the word *parousia* itself. The four occurrences in Matthew 24 all fall into this category.

In 24:3 *parousia* must refer to Jesus' coming, since the disciples ask for a sign. We could hardly envision them as asking for a sign of His being present. In 24:27, 37, and 39 the *parousia* of Christ is compared to things that occur suddenly (lightning and the flood). A continuous presence is not something sudden. Thus, staying is not in view in the Matthew 24 occurrences.

The author has committed the linguistic error of *illegitimate totality transfer*, in which meanings of a word in various occurrences and contexts are all poured into one particular occurrence.[1] An example of this would be saying that *horn* means "a projection from an animal's head," "the end of a crescent," "a brass or other wind instrument," "a noise-making device on a vehicle," "one of the alternatives in a dilemma" and "a telephone" all at the same time and in all occurrences. We can see the formulation of this error quite clearly in the following statement:

> *Parousia* (coming) is derived from two Greek words, *para* meaning *with* and *ousia* meaning *being*. *Parousia*, then denotes two things: an arrival and a consequent presence with. (p. 217)

First, there is a non sequitur here. The fact that *parousia* is made from *para* ("with") and *ousia* ("being") does not lead to the conclusion that it denotes arrival and presence. In addition, in talking about the two parts of *parousia*, the author has committed another linguistic error, that of trying to determine the meaning of a word from its history. This is the *etymological fallacy*.[2] Only rarely can we get an accurate picture of the meaning of a word from the history of its formation.

The problem we face here is that sometimes *parousia* refers to a coming and sometimes to a presence. But each occurrence must be examined individually. That sometimes people come and stay, does not mean that coming and staying are always linked, either in life in general or in regard to the return of the Lord Jesus Christ. The author has provided no sound linguistic evidence for his assertion that Christ comes and stays.

The author asserts that the Lord's coming is consistently described as a singular event. That is true. But portrayal as a single event does not mean He stays. Two comings (the first to die and the second in glory) are portrayed as singular in Malachi 3:1-4, yet they are separated by over 1,950 years, with Christ being absent during the whole time!

Overlooking Differences

The author's challenge (p. 223) to prove two comings is made on the basis of overlooking biblical distinctions. He never deals significantly with the differences between 1 Thessalonians 4 (a coming for believers to meet them in the clouds) and passages such as Zechariah 14 (a coming to the earth on the Mount of Olives in power and glory). Compare how the Bible describes the two events:

	1 Thessalonians 4	Zechariah 14
Place	In the Air	To the Earth
Purpose	Take Believers	Judge Nations and Establish the Kingdom
Object	The Church	Israel
Character	A Comfort	Bring Judgment
Side Effects	No Changes in the Earth	Topographical Changes

No "Return" in 1 Thessalonians 4

If 1 Thessalonians 4 is describing a coming that is entirely singular, why doesn't Paul give any information there on the "return in glory" (the author's words)?

The Language of Daniel

Matthew 24:30-31 and 25:30 describe Jesus' return in language unmistakably drawn from Daniel 7. In both Matthew and Daniel the immediate result is the inauguration of the Kingdom. The events of 1 Thessalonians 4 (the Rapture) are quite different, yet the author lumps the two events together, without any attempt to show why they do not use the same language.

What is Jesus Doing?

The most crucial feature of the collapsing of the two comings is the lack of ability on the author's part to portray what Jesus is doing while He is present. Here is what he says:

> This coming commences *before* the end of the seventieth week, and is consummated after the end of the seventieth week (Rev. 19:11). (p. 110)

He gives no Scripture for this. Where is Jesus and what is He doing? The silence on this is deafening! He can give no information because there is no Scripture to support his position.

Circular Reasoning

The author asserts that the use of *parousia* demonstrates the fact of the Rapture's inclusion in the second coming. But he never demonstrates this from a discussion of the usage of the word in the New Testament, analyzing the possible meanings of the word and its use in particular contexts. Instead, his points are made on the basis of his conclusion—that the Rapture and the second advent are only one event. He thus assumes ahead of time what he wants to prove. Once again we see circular reasoning. Yet he includes the "arrival-and-consequent-presence" meaning of *parousia* in a list of "salient facts" (p. 229).

The "Saints" of 1 Thessalonians 3:13

If taken at face value, 1 Thessalonians 3:13 describes Christ's coming in glory to the earth, the second advent, since in the Rapture Christ comes *for* saints and later comes *with* them.

85

> To the end he may establish your hearts unblamable in holiness before God, even our Father, at the coming of our Lord Jesus Christ with all his saints.

The dictionary form of the word translated here "saints" is *hagios*.

Such a coming with believers contradicts the author's scheme of events, so he must make it something other than the second advent. Therefore, he asserts that the word *hagios* refers to angels. Let's take a careful look at the word in Paul's writings. Usage in nearby texts and in other writings by the same author are the most determinative factors for understanding the sense of a word or phrase. What do we learn concerning *hagios*? In no instance is there any clear use by Paul or anyone else in the New Testament of *hagios* referring to an angel. Yet the author boldly asserts,

> "Saints" in this verse is an unfortunate and inappropriate translation. "Saints" in this verse does not refer to believers. The Greek word *hagios* should be translated *holy ones* and is a reference to angelic beings. (p. 218)

It is a telling fact that the author gives absolutely no support of any kind for his translation—no commentator, no lexicon, no grammar. Simply saying something dogmatically does not make it so. Once again we see circular arguing.

The End of the Age

In giving the Great Commission in Matthew 28:18-20, Jesus promises to be with His disciples "to the very end of the age." The author tries to show that references in Matthew to "the end of the age" and "the end" point to a time within the seventieth week and prior to the end of the Day of the Lord (p. 230). Thus, he asserts,

> If the Great Commission of the church is to evangelize the world up to the end, then the church must enter the seventieth week of the book of Daniel in order to fulfill its holy calling . . . . (p. 228)

In citing passages that refer to the phrase "the end," the author lists 1 Corinthians 15:24 (p. 228). A careful reading of 1 Corinthians 15:24-28 shows that the "end" of verse 24 must be *after* the Millennial Kingdom of Christ, since the Son first rules on the earth (v. 25, quoting from Ps. 110:1, and v. 27, quoting from Ps. 8:6, both Kingdom-rule prophecies). It is *after* His Kingdom that the Lord Jesus Christ hands His authority over to the Father.

Age in Matthew

In discussing the use of *age* in Matthew, the author says,

> The suggestion that the "end" or "end of the age" in these passages do not refer to the same "end" ought not to be taken seriously by those who honor God's Word. (p. 228)

This is nothing other than the fallacy of *argumentation by ridicule* and is something that appears often in the book. Yet he can also say,

> I plea for tolerance in discussions related to the timing of Christ's second coming and the Rapture of the church. (p. 280)

I leave it to the reader to compare these two statements.

Conclusion

The pre-wrath position errs in its treatment of *parousia* and its understanding of the biblical practice of merging multiple, separate, future events. It overlooks key details of New Testament "return" passages, cannot account for what Jesus is doing during His stay, and makes other errors concerning events that it connects His coming. Its collapsing of the Rapture and second advent fails.

NOTES

1. See, for example, Moises Silva, *An Introduction to Lexical Semantics* (Grand Rapids: Zondervan, 1983), p. 25.

2. Silva, p. 39.

12

Summary

THROUGH AN EXAMINATION of the author's attention to facts, language, context, and logic, we have shown that there are major flaws in the position presented in *The Pre-Wrath Rapture of the Church*. Here are the primary conclusions we have seen:

1. Wrath begins before the cosmic disturbances and during the author's Tribulation and is not exclusive to the Day of the Lord.

2. There are blessings during the Day of the Lord.

3. It is not necessarily true that the Tribulation is shortened to less than three and one-half years.

4. The seals of Revelation 6 do not describe eternal security for the Church.

5. Cosmic disturbances cannot be identified exclusively with the time just prior to the author's posited Rapture and thus do not signal the beginning of his Day of the Lord.

6. There is not one single eschatological trumpet, a "last trump," that signals the Rapture and the start of the Day of the Lord.

7. The multitude of Revelation 7 is never said to be the true Church.

8. The account of Noah provides no support for a Rapture that occurs on the very same day on which the Day of the Lord begins.

9. The apostasy or falling away of 2 Thessalonians 2 cannot be identified with an exclusively Jewish rebellion.

10. The two witnesses appear too late in Revelation for the author's timetable.

11. The first beast of Revelation 13 is not a king who raises himself or is raised by Satan.

12. Daniel 12:1 does not teach that Michael stands aside or desists from helping Israel.

13. *Parousia* cannot be used to prove that the Lord Jesus Christ raptures the Church and then remains on the scene through the Day of the Lord. The Rapture and the second coming are two distinguishable events with different purposes and different outcomes.

14. The book of Revelation contradicts the author's chronology of events.

15. There is no practical difference between the trials of the author's Tribulation period and those of the Day of the Lord, nor between the difficulties for Israel during the Tribulation period and the Day of the Lord.

Individually or in combination, these show the errors in the author's announced goals and theses, which appear to be the following:

1. "The objective of this volume is to demonstrate that the Day of the Lord is the time of divine wrath." (p. 35)

2. "The Rapture of the church will occur immediately prior to the beginning of the Day of the Lord." (p. 60)

3. "The Day of the Lord commences sometime within the second half of the seventieth week." (p. 60)

4. "The cosmic disturbances associated with the sixth seal will signal the approach of the Day of the Lord." (p. 60)

5. "The Day of the Lord will begin with the opening of the seventh seal (Rev. 8:1)." (p. 60)

The Author's Methodology and the "One Text" Challenge

We have noted several times that the author's position is arrived at by linking together several lines of argument, each of which is weak in itself. The total argument is quite complicated. However, he challenges pretribulationists to cite one specific biblical text that explicitly teaches pretribulation rapturism. Apparently he does not realize that, as he presents it, his own position is made from various texts and is not taught in one passage or verse. He also says that the lack of one particular text proving the pretribulation Rapture means there "simply is no explicit exegetical evidence" for it (p. 280). But it is not necessary to have a doctrine taught in one particular text for it to be valid. Remember, the Trinity is not taught in "one text"! It is an orthodox doctrine that is built from several texts and lines of evidence. Most major doctrines are built on conclusions drawn from many portions of Scripture. Argumentation using this kind of challenge proves nothing.

Questions the Reader Is Likely to Ask

1. The author says that he may not have dotted all his *i*'s or crossed all his *t*'s, yet the basic tenets of the position will not be overthrown (p. 292). While there may be some problems with the pre-wrath Rapture, doesn't it have enough truth to it to make it viable?

Answer: The author argues by joining many links with inherent flaws. The whole chain sounds good by virtue of repetition, but the basic theses are not supported by the facts.

2. What about problems with the pretribulation Rapture. Doesn't *The Pre-Wrath Rapture* show that the position is false?

Answer: This book has not attempted to present the pretribulation position or to answer accusations against it, but, rather, to assess the pre-wrath position on its own merits, with regard to its logic and attention to facts, context and language. There are some problems that need attention in the pretribulation position, but that doesn't mean it should be thrown out, as the author suggests. Furthermore, few, if any, pretribulationists would assert that they have all the answers about the Rapture and related events. Just because students of the Bible who hold a particular position don't agree on all its fine points doesn't mean the position as a whole is wrong.

3. Few writers express such sincerity, conviction, and emotion in their work as does the author of *The Pre-Wrath Rapture*. Isn't this evidence

that God has led the author uniquely and that the latter is speaking truth in accord with Scripture?

Answer: Sincerity, conviction, and emotion are all valuable in their place, but by themselves they prove nothing. There are many sincere people who deny the saving work of Christ and are on their way to a Christless eternity, yet the Christian would hardly say they must be right because of their sincerity. Any position must be evaluated on the basis of its logic and attention to the facts.

4. Doesn't the pre-wrath Rapture really offer an effective challenge to the lethargy of Christians today?

Answer: The New Testament is always positive concerning the effect of prophecy on the life of a Christian, who is to look forward to righteousness, because it will be our full possession. Believers are not told to be righteous now because life will get harder. See 2 Peter 3; Philippians 2:20; Hebrews 11:1-40.

5. You argue against the position of the pre-wrath Rapture. Isn't this attacking the author and using the *ad hominem* argument?

Answer: No. I do not attack his circumstances, background or motives. It is entirely fair and absolutely necessary to show how he handles evidence and presents his case.

6. You attack the author's logic. Do you think he is illogical or incoherent?

Answer: "Illogical" is not a term that applies in this evaluation. It usually means "rambling." I have said that the author doesn't conform to the principles of formal and informal logic. I have not said he is incoherent.

Appendix: Just for the Record

THERE ARE MANY ERRORS of fact, language, context, and logic in *The Pre-Wrath Rapture* that have not been mentioned. These are not simply typographical errors.

The author admits that he is not a scholar, yet claims that his book is scholarly (p. 34). However, a nonscholar cannot produce a scholarly book. I am not saying he is not a scholar. That is his statement. Nor am I saying that a nonscholar cannot write or speak truth; he certainly can. But it is fair to see if what the author writes meets the tests of scholarship, some of which I have described in the previous chapters.

Thus, while the following errors do not directly affect the basic thesis of the book, they should be mentioned, because mistakes of this kind are incompatible with normally accepted scholarship.

Logical Errors

1. Irrelevant Data

In arguing against the pretribulation Rapture, the author mentions several well-known Christian leaders of past generations, indicating that they were not pretribulational (p. 54). Actually, some of them were not even premillennial, so mentioning them is irrelevant. It's like saying that 200 million Americans aren't pretribulational, so it must be a suspicious position.

2. Disagreement versus Error

The author argues that existing differences in interpretation mean that all the positions are wrong.

> The ongoing conflict between the opposing views, the glaring problems, and frequently heard statements like, "I

don't know what to believe," or "I'm a posttribulationist because it seems to have fewer problems than pretribulationism," and not infrequently, "I'm a pretribulationist, but I never preach on it," strongly suggest that the prevailing views are fatally flawed—and that a fresh new examination not only should be welcomed but warmly encouraged. (p. 59)

This is once again the fallacy of the false dilemma: too few choices. He only gives the choice that all are wrong ("fatally flawed"), whereas another option is that one of the positions is right. Ongoing disagreement between parties does not mean both are wrong. The author is a premillennialist. Amillennialists and premillennialists have been on opposite sides of some issues for many years. By his logic we would have to say that both are wrong and toss them out! But I doubt very much that he would be willing to do that.

3. Biasing the Reader

The logical fallacy of *poisoning the well* consists of disallowing an unwanted response from an opponent before he has had a chance to speak. When the author predicts the failure of all future critics of his position, he is biasing the reader before the reader can hear what the critics say (pp. 292-93). This may be effective argumentation, but it is not good logic.

4. Emotions versus Facts

The author frequently demonstrates the fallacy of the *appeal to emotion*, which involves attempting to get support for a position by arousing people's feelings. The extensive personal presentation of chapter 1 contains many examples of this. It may be an accurate record of his wrestling with the issues, but it should not be accepted as a substitute for logical argumentation of his case and presentation of biblical facts.

5. Looking for Compassion

The fallacy of the *appeal to pity* seeks the reader's compassion or concern. The following statement exemplifies this:

> I write at considerable personal cost—not as an ivory-tower theologian who may theorize but live apart from his theories....
>
> If I am wrong, ten thousand angels arguing my cause would not make it right, and I will have played the fool. (p. 35)

6. Bandwagon and Unknowable Facts

The *appeal to the people* fallacy, also known more popularly as the *bandwagon argument*, attempts to sway people to a position by appealing to their desire to be part of a group or to have something that other people have. Here is an example:

> Within two years many men will be teaching the prewrath Rapture. Within five years it will be a recognized position. And, if God pleases, within fifteen years it will become a major position of the believing church—if God gives that many years. (p. 293)

This quote also demonstrates the fallacy of the *appeal to unknowable facts*. The author's predicted acceptance is something that no one can know now, and so cannot support his argument.

Linguistic Errors

1. The author claims that the Greek word *parousia* is pronounced "pa-ROOzee-a" (p. 215). He has capitalized the second syllable as the one he thinks is accented. As a matter of linguistic fact, which can be verified in any standard Greek lexicon, the stress is on the third syllable, not the second. In addition, the Greek *sigma* (*s* in the transliteration) is never to be pronounced as *z* but as equivalent to the English *s*. The correct representation would be pa-roo-SEE-a.

2. The author says that the Greek word equivalent to English *mark* is *stigmata* (p. 137). *Mark* is actually a singular form, while *stigmata* is plural.

3. There are two acceptable transliterations for the Greek word translated "revelation" or "unveiling": *apokalypsis* or *apokalupsis*. The

author has the word *apokolipse*, which actually contains three errors (p. 286).

4. The author asserts (p. 53) that the source of *rapture* is the Latin word *rapere*, meaning "rapid." Once again, as a matter of linguistic fact, *rapere* is the infinitive form of a verb (*rapid* is an adjective) and means "to seize," "to plunder" or "to hurry (someone or something) along." *Rapture* is from the Latin word *raptus*, which means "seizing," and which is a participle made from *rapere*.

Scripture Index

21:1	40
21:9	54
21:17	41
22:3	41
21:27	41
22:3	41
27:64	72

Subject Index

This book is available from:

BF Press
P.O. Box L-601
Langhorne, PA 19047